December 2018

Jeff,

About a marine, to another marine.

Happy holidays!

Bill

CHUIE, THE MAJOR

Chuie, The Major

THE STORY OF

ARTHUR H. TURNER

A HERO

AT BELLEAU WOOD AND SOISSONS

AND A MARINE

IN AND OUT OF WAR

William D. Turner

SNOWMASS VILLAGE, COLORADO

Chuie, The Major
By William Dow Turner

Copyright © 2018 by William D. Turner

ISBN 978-0-9964454-7-4

DESIGN & MAPS | CURT CARPENTER © 2018

PRINTED IN THE UNITED STATES

DOW TURNER
Box 6065 · Snowmass Village, Colorado 81615

CONTENTS

DEDICATION

For all the descendants of

ARTHUR TURNER

... 17 so far and counting.

AUTHOR'S NOTE

I KNEW AND REMEMBER ARTHUR TURNER, my father's father, during the last two decades of his life and the second two decades of mine. We visited him and my grandmother every few years at their home in Brooklyn, New York, and in the 1950's, he took me on the subway to a Brooklyn Dodgers game and also aboard an aircraft carrier docked at the Brooklyn Navy Yard. Later, when I lived in Manhattan after college, I spent a bit more time with him. He was blind then, and I would walk with him around his neighborhood, visiting shops—once shopping for a new red tip for his cane. (As a result, I became acclimated to helping blind folks cross streets in Manhattan, wondering why so few others would step forward to help.)

But in my fog of memory, what stands out as a central part of his persona—from our first meetings to his funeral service—is his wooden leg. There was the childhood fascination of seeing and tapping on the hardwood substitute for his left shin and foot, and obeying his commands to 'kick it hard'—an experience shared among his grandchildren. And the curious ritual of putting on his leg each morning and having to tie only one shoe.

We knew from our family that he had lost his leg in World War I in France and that he was a war hero. Everyone outside his immediate family addressed and referred to him as 'Major.' His closest relatives—with a vocabulary rich with pet names for family members—called him Chuie (pronounced 'shewy').

Through his sons (my father and uncle), we have an assortment of photographs and artifacts. But, I did not know many details, especially of his career as a Marine Corps officer, which lasted intermittently from 1913 to 1946. Nor, I must admit, did I know much about World War I (WWI), beyond the basics.

So, a couple years ago, I set out to 'research' Arthur Turner's life, concentrating on what he did during WWI. Facilitated by the Internet, there is also a cache of good books and video documentaries with detailed descriptions of the war's events and even his Marine Corps unit's activities. But, those sources had their limits when it came to following his day-to-day movements during the war, let alone the rest of his nearly 30 years as a Marine, let alone his extra-Marine life.

In July of 2017, I applied to the National Personnel Records Center in St. Louis for my grandfather's service record. And, that fall, my wife Paula and I joined an old-friend couple on a tour of WWI battlefields between Paris and Ypres, Belgium, which includes the region where he had fought. This trip was an enlightening tutorial. Besides hosting wonderful memorials, museums, and shrines devoted to the war's local events a century ago, the rural countryside had changed little, with the Allied and German trenches and their surrounding fields, hamlets, and graveyards still echoing the four years of fighting there so long ago.

In March 2018, 550 pages of military records arrived—yes, eight months after the request. Although it contained only Marine

Corps related documents, and although the pages were in nearly random order (not chronological, often collated backwards, and never stapled), the material was gold for my hunt. The massive missive contains orders, postings, fitness and medical reports, as well as correspondence between the Major and Marine Corps top brass, and among the brass themselves.

Combining and reconciling all this with family letters and memories, and with the various reports about the war and his Marine Corps units, has produced a narrative—albeit incomplete—of Arthur Turner's life, at least in terms of when and where he was, what he was doing, and how his life unfolded.

However, it has left us with many unanswered questions when it comes to how and why he made many of his life's most important decisions and, more generally, what he thought about things. Readers of the story are left to infer his motives, ambitions, likes and dislikes, and innate feelings. Many of his capabilities, and even values, become clear by virtue of what he did and how he behaved. But, owing to few and small writings in his own hand, we must infer a lot.

An attempt has been made to present his story in the all-important context of World War I, which set the trajectory for Arthur Turner's adult life. But, although the war was long and complicated, and requires some description for context, I fear the amount of that description about the war contained herein may be a bit excessive. If so, blame it on the author's desire and attempt to remind himself continually about the view of world events from Arthur Turner's eyes. ✪

—W D T | July 19, 2018

ACKNOWLEDGMENTS

―――――――――――

T HE STARTING POINT—beyond my own slim recollections about my grandfather and anecdotes passed on to
me by my parents—was several drawers accumulated by my
mother (wife of Chuie and Dorothy Turner's son Donald). There
were a few photo albums, correspondence, newspaper articles,
and other material alluding to many of our ancestors, including
grandfather Arthur.

As already cited, the military records for Major Arthur H.
Turner, provided by the National Personnel Records Center,
proved invaluable as a skeleton for tracking his career as a
Marine. Despite the longer-than-anticipated wait, the process
for accessing the records was simple and straightforward, and
represents a valuable Government resource for anyone delving
into a soldier's history.

Also already mentioned, the eight-day *New York Times* tour,
"Remembering the Great War (1914-1918)," provided a 'kick-the-
tires' led by two experienced guides, covering the four years
of war in that area of France, including those battles in which
Arthur participated and helped win.

Important and gratifying were the anecdotes, additional arti-facts, records, and general perceptions about grandfather Arthur provided by family members who knew him or of him. His grandson and my cousin Charles Turner, who lived with Arthur and Dorothy in their Brooklyn apartment in the summer of 1962 and then for 14 months in 1967-68, was particu-larly helpful, relating war and personal stories. Charlie also pro-vided images of the Major's medals. Charlie's sister, Ellen Turner Scott, was similarly helpful, as the keeper of their mother's fine and extensive trove of family histories, including grandfather Arthur. Ellen spent hours digging through the trove and for-warding relevant items.

Platt Arnold and Bill Butler, two of Arthur's sister's grandchil-dren, who grew up near Wilkes-Barre, Pennsylvania, supplied anecdotes and stories about Chuie from their memory of him and from his sister Edith, with whom Platt and Bill were very close.

My warm thanks go to Charlie, Ellen, Platt, and Bill for their help.

Finally, thanks to Curt Carpenter, who's editing, design, and publishing assistance made this volume possible. ✪

ESTABLISHED 1879

C. S. TURNER COMPANY

IMPORTERS OF

Teas, Coffees and Spices

1321 Walnut Street,   Philadelphia, Pa.

MILLS

South and Pennsylvania Ave,   Wilkes-Barre, Pa.

PART ONE

Growing Up in Industrial America

The son of an immigrant entrepreneur
in a Pennsylvania coal town, Arthur Turner
becomes an Ivy League educated engineer.

W ith the middle name "Hubesty," how could his life not be noteworthy? Arthur Hubesty Turner was born in Wilkes-Barre, Pennsylvania, on October 13, 1887, the son of Delphine Huber and Charles Simpson Turner. His mother was born on a farm near Chinchilla, Pennsylvania (near Scranton) in 1869, and married Charles in 1884 when she was 15 years old. Charles was born in York, England, in 1857, and was the youngest of eight surviving children. Figuring he was not destined to inherit much from his father's wholesale food business in Leeds, Charles emigrated from Shoreditch, Middlesex, England, as a tea taster and settled in Wilkes-Barre. He began importing tea and other foodstuffs, and then established a wholesale tea, coffee, spice and flavoring extract business, with a retail store and warehouse and railroad siding facilities on Pennsylvania Avenue. The company's importing operation was based in Philadelphia.

Regarding Arthur's middle name, there are a few references to folks in England with that name and at least one such surname in Ohio. But, no Hubesty links could be found to Arthur Turner's ancestry, and the word has proved exceedingly rare. An 1861 newspaper article contains "hubesty" as a misspelling of "honesty," and there is a reference to an Internet domain name "hubesty," owned by a Besty Hu!

A fence top of 40-inch high iron statues of Mr. Peanut bordered the company headquarters building in Wilkes-Barre, Pennsylvania.

FAMILY AND WILKES-BARRE

THE FAMILY PROSPERED as the anthracite coal-mining town grew in the last part of the 19th century. Wilkes-Barre had a population of 38,000 in the 1890s and was to be the family 'hometown' through the 20th century. In addition to booming as a coal town, Wilkes-Barre saw the local entrepreneur Fred M. Kirby combine with a friend to open a local five-and-dime store in 1884, which launched the nationwide F.M. Kirby and F.W. Woolworth chain stores. In 1912, the two companies, having a combined 400 stores, merged and continued expanding under the Woolworth name. It was rumored that the two founders flipped a coin for the name, with Woolworth winning, but Woolworth's was in any case much larger, with about 300 stores to Kirby's 100. It was stipulated that Fred's first store in Wilkes-Barre would forever retain the F.M. Kirby name, and it did.

The city also was the home of Planters Peanut Company, founded there by two Italian immigrants in 1906. Their first headquarters building was bordered by statues of the company's top-hatted Mr. Peanut, which was adopted from a sketch submitted by a local schoolboy in a 1916 contest for a Planters brand icon.

But Wilkes-Barre was first and foremost a coal mining town. About 1970, when grandfather Arthur was again living in Wilkes-Barre, I paid a visit to the local Social Security office on his behalf. Standing in line at the service counter, I noticed a six-inch thick book that looked like some kind of manual. Towards the center of the big volume, there was a section that stood out, where the pages were rumpled, discolored and frayed from what appeared to be constant use. When I got to the front of the line, I asked the service representative about the book, and she said it was the Federal Social Security regulations. But, what is that section that's so heavily used, I asked. She replied, "Oh, that's the part that covers black lung disease."

Arthur was the middle child, his sister Edith (nicknamed 'Mothe') being born a year earlier, and brother Charles Franklin (called 'Pammie' by his siblings, 'Pat' by others) nine years later in 1896. They called Arthur 'Chuie' all his life. The family lived at 188 West River Street in Wilkes-Barre, and they were active members of the St. Stephens Episcopal Church in town.

Arthur attended the Harry Hillman Academy on Terrace Street in Wilkes-Barre, only a two-minute walk from home. Opening in 1884, Hillman was a private grammar and high school aimed at providing a classical education and preparing young well-to-do boys of the Wyoming Valley for Ivy League colleges. The $150 tuition was affordable by only the area's top-earning families, which signals the success of Arthur's father and the family business. The school's total student body never surpassed 150 in those days, taught by a total of nine or ten teachers. Arthur graduated in June of 1904, after attending the Academy eleven years.

In 1897, ten-year-old Arthur visited Paris with his family and a cousin, Lucy, who traveled from Wortley, between Leeds and Sheffield, England, to join them on the trip in France. This traveling is another indication that the Turner family was prospering with its wholesale business in the States, as was Lucy's family in their large wholesale grocery and sugar brokering business in Leeds.

This brick house at 188 West River Street remained the Turner Family home in Wilkes-Barre, from before Arthur was born in the 1880s, until his father passed away in 1944.

COLLEGE AND FIRST JOBS

A FTER GRADUATING FROM HIGH SCHOOL at the early age of 16 in 1904, Arthur attended Princeton University—120 miles to the southeast in New Jersey—where he took up civil engineering and joined the fencing team, among other activities. He was one of 202 freshmen in the Princeton School of Science, living at 33 Edwards Place in the town. By the start of his sophomore year, his class of science majors had shrunk by 25% to 151 students. He was forever designated a member of the Princeton class of 1908.

Following his sophomore year at Princeton, Arthur transferred to the Massachusetts Institute of Technology (MIT)—'Boston Tech' as he called it then. And, after three years at MIT, he graduated with a Bachelor of Science degree in Civil Engineering on June 8, 1909. It is not known why he left Princeton, or why he apparently took five years to earn his degree.

After graduation, Arthur went to work as an engineer for Baldwin Locomotive Works in Atlanta, Georgia. Headquartered in Philadelphia, BLW was the largest and most influential manufacturer of steam railroad locomotives in the world. In 1911, he was elected a junior member of the American Society of Civil Engineers.

In January of 1912, he had joined with other local MIT graduates to form an Atlanta-based alumni association. By that same year, he was working as Assistant Engineer at the Southern Ferro Concrete Company, an Atlanta-based pioneer in the development and building use of reinforced concrete. Either with those companies or separately, he also worked briefly in Philadelphia and Detroit, presumably as an engineer. ✪

U.S.S. NEBRASKA
MARINE GUARD

E.A. Hodge
Boston
#1

PART TWO

Fits and Starts
to Join the Great War

Driven to participate in the war in Europe,
Arthur joins the Marines as an officer,
serves two years in the Caribbean, resigns out of frustration,
but rejoins as the U.S. enters the war.

A EUROPEAN WORLD

A T THE TURN OF THE 20TH CENTURY, Europe was flourishing from economic growth driven by the continuing industrial revolution, the extension of the ruling hereditary European monarchies into far-flung empires, and an evolving balance of power among those empires. Europe contained one-quarter of the world's population, and it was prospering.

At the same time, however, the rise of mass socialist movements and political insecurities within European nations, and distrusted and often conflicting alliances among the countries and empires, had created a tinderbox. The major powers of Europe built up large, expensive militaries, and the chances for accidental or purposeful crises and conflicts were increasing by the day. Examples of belligerent actions and conflicts between 1909 and 1912 included German-backed Austria-Hungary annexation of Bosnia-Herzegovina; a German gunboat arriving in Tangier, Morocco; Italy declaring war on Turkey over claims in Libya; and the beginning of a Balkan War between Turkey and the Balkan league of countries. Late in 1912, Britain and France agreed to share naval forces and responsibilities across and around Europe.

JOINING UP

AS A SLIDE TOWARD WAR in Europe appeared imminent, young engineer Arthur Turner thought America should be allying with Britain and France, which shared America's values and traditions, and which opposed Germany and the other offensive empires. Upset with America's declared neutrality and reluctance to join in—and feeling personally compelled to get involved—he applied to the United States Marine Corps officer program in mid-1912, unwittingly embarking on a military career that would last more than three decades.

His motives may also have included disillusionment with engineering or business in general; interest in France, the United Kingdom, and Europe sparked from his earlier visits; or the influence of his UK relatives. Why the Marine Corps in particular, is a mystery—perhaps it offered the quickest, most certain path to officer status.

GAINING HIS COMMISSION

ARTHUR TOOK THE REQUIRED EXAMINATIONS for officer in October of 1912, before a Marine Examination

Board at the Marine Barracks in Washington, D.C. He passed all subjects, "attaining a higher mark in probable efficiency and a higher general average than any other of the twenty-nine candidates who completed the exam at that time." Physically, he stood 5' 5 ¾" tall (probably a slightly understated measurement) and weighed 117 pounds. His vision was found to be defective at 5/20, but was deemed acceptable when "corrected by glasses," with a 19/20 right eye and an 18/20 left eye. As a result, he was recommended for commission as a second lieutenant.

As the recommendation worked its way up the top levels of the American military for approval that fall, Arthur informed the Marine Corps that he would in fact be unable to accept that commission: "Shortly after receiving this good news, I was compelled, on account of family affairs, to put aside my own personal wishes in the matter and enter commercial business necessitating my informing you of my regret that it would be impossible for me to accept a commission."

Whatever the family business or affairs were, less than three months later his situation had changed, and on January 18, 1913 he wrote Marine Corps Headquarters again: "The necessity of my continuing in business has now been removed and as I am very very anxious to obtain a commission in the Corps, I would like to know if it is in any way possible for me to set aside my former rejection, accept the appointment without further examination and enter the Marine Officers' School immediately." It was, and he did.

He was appointed a second lieutenant on January 30, 1913, and reported for duty. His formal commission, retroactive to January 30, and signed by President William Howard Taft, is dated March 3, 1913. (That was Taft's last day in office.)

Marine Corps commission, signed by President Taft

Lieutenant Turner spent his first year in the Marine Corps—from March 1913 to April 1914—at the Marine Officers' School in Norfolk, Virginia "for duty and instruction". He completed his course work and did very well, including placing first in his class in an "intensive four-month course covering bookkeeping, accounting and post exchange accounts."

At the end of his course program, Arthur remained based at the Marine Barracks at Norfolk and was to "serve honorably both ashore and afloat" over the next year.

SHIPPING ABROAD

THE MARINE CORPS, although old (first formed in 1775) and proud, was in 1914 a small and underappreciated force. As part of the Navy, its mission was primarily to provide shipboard detachments to deploy ashore as infantry when needed, and was considered by many to be an anachronism of the days of sail.

Navy ships were being sent to Mexico that spring to protect American interests during the Mexican revolution. On April 23, Arthur embarked on the *Morro Castle* at Philadelphia for expeditionary duty at Vera Cruz, Mexico, attached to the First Regiment, First Brigade, Marines. He disembarked at Vera Cruz six days later and was transferred—or 'detached'—to the Army there. Seven months later, as the American forces withdrew from Vera Cruz, he sailed back to Philadelphia on the *Denver*.

TAKEN DOWN A NOTCH

DURING HIS TOUR OF DUTY at Vera Cruz, Lieutenant Turner inquired, or complained, about the failure of the School to recommend him for a Certificate of Graduation, in spite of his strong performance and the completion of his courses.

Yes, he had 'earned' several infractions and write-ups while at the school earlier in 1914, including one for returning 30 minutes late from a Saturday leave (suspended 10 days); another for carrying on a classroom conversation after being warned not to (5-day suspension); and another for riding on horseback beyond the base outpost "at a gallop" to Punta Gorda (no leave for 15 days). But, the fitness reports by Colonel James Mahoney, the officer in charge of the School, and by Major General Commandant George Barnett, were scathing and went far deeper than the handful of transgressions. In Barnett's words, sent to Arthur on May 12:

> "Colonel Mahoney, in summing up the unfavorable portions of the report, states that you show a lack of judgment, that you are conceited, inclined to be insubordinate and are lacking in frankness; that you have great ability, which fact makes the defects mentioned all the more notable; and that you are indolent and apparently are not trying to improve. I regret that your commanding officer found it necessary to make such a report as the one referred to, and you are admonished to ... take such steps as will obviate attention being called to your shortcomings by your commanding officer."

Again from General Barnett, on July 28:

> "In a communication received from the officer in charge of Marine Officers' School, dated July 10, 1914, in relation to your failure to be recommended for a certificate of graduation from said School, the following statement appears:

'...in my opinion the failure of Second Lieutenant Arthur H. Turner, M.C., to attain a certificate of graduation was due to want of application, and to unreliability and offensive manner of performing duty, both with senior officers and enlisted men.'

I deeply regret that you should begin your active career with such a blur on your record, and I deem it my duty to bring to your attention the fact that a report of this character, unless much improvement on your part is displayed in the near future, will very strongly militate against you as an officer, and when considered by a board, before which you will appear for examination for the next higher grade, will, in my opinion, properly be ascribed either to absolute indifference on your part as to the requirements of an officer, or to such a mental condition as will demonstrate your incompetency. This opinion on my part will no doubt be considered by the board as very unfavorable testimony in your case, and it is therefore incumbent on you to so change your procedure as to cause me to modify my opinion. I am willing to believe that perhaps your youth may in some degree be responsible for the above outlined condition, but it is in no way accepted by me as an excuse, and you are therefore warned that unless marked improvement be shown in the near future I will consider it incumbent to lay your case before the Department so that the necessary disciplinary and remedial action may be taken."

Perhaps this type of message was a planned and common part of Marine Corps officer training and toughening at the time, no matter what the officer's performance at the School. This is unlikely, however, as these reports remain in Arthur's Marine Corps file a century later. (And, frankly, the underlying attitudes are not unlike some recollections of Arthur Turner by this author decades later.)

The superior and aloof attitude and cavalier behavior may well have been an accurate portrait of Lieutenant Turner at the time. In the previous five years, 26-year-old Arthur had graduated from a top university with an engineering degree, worked for a major company or two, scored the highest rating on Marine Corps Officer examinations, been accepted into the Marine officer program twice, and probably was a 'quick study' during his courses.

In any case, the nature and wording of the reprimand certainly would have planted in Arthur the fear of failure and potential rejection from the Marine Corps. There is no record of a response from him, but he was around that time "directed" by Barnett "to submit to the Officer in Charge...not later than April 30, 1915, an essay of between four and seven thousand words on some professional subject." The subject of Barnett's note was "Graduation thesis from Marine Officers' School."

Although it is unclear if this essay was meant to offset his earlier indiscretions, Arthur submitted his thesis—on "Military Topography"—on April 20, 1915. It is also unclear whether he ever received his Graduation Certificate. But, no other similar criticisms and admonitions were seen again in his military file over the next 30 years. Needless to say, Chuie did not share the 1914 written reprimands with his family.

ABOARD THE *DENVER* on his way from Vera Cruz back to Philadelphia on November 25, 1914, Arthur Turner received orders to report to Mare Island Naval Shipyard five weeks hence, in order to sail from San Francisco for duty in Guam and the Pacific. However, a few days after docking in Philadelphia, Arthur found another Second Lieutenant who wanted duty in the Pacific, and the two of them got the swap approved, allowing Arthur to remain in Philadelphia. But not for long.

On January 4 of the new year 1915, Arthur was ordered to join the Marine detachment on board the battleship U.S.S. *Nebraska*, shipping to Guantanamo Bay, Cuba. On the *Nebraska*, Arthur served "under that fine splendid Commander Arthur MacArthur, U.S.N., older brother of the famous General Douglas MacArthur." (Eventually a Navy Captain, Arthur MacArthur would die in 1923 at the age of 47 from a burst appendix and the ensuing peritonitis. Some years later, Arthur Turner, then also aged 47, similarly suffered a burst appendix, but because penicillin had become available for treatment of peritonitis, he survived.)

Shortly after arriving in Cuba, Arthur transferred to the armored cruiser U.S.S. *Montana*, for "temporary expeditionary service beyond the seas." The *Montana* had landed Marines in Haiti to prevent rioting there, following abdication of the country's president, and also had taken part in the U.S. occupation of Vera Cruz. Lieutenant Turner was in charge of the *Montana*'s Marine complement, but, by that time, the ship's role was primarily patrolling Haiti, Cuba, and the east coast of Mexico. After only a few weeks on the *Montana*, Turner returned to his Marine base at Guantanamo, and to the *Nebraska*.

The battleship U.S.S. *Nebraska,* captained by Arthur MacArthur, underway off New York City.

WATCHING THE WAR WITH FRUSTRATION

FROM THE SUMMER OF 1914 through to the spring of 1915, Lieutenant Turner no doubt followed with interest and frustration the continued escalation of conflict in Europe, culminating in the assassination of Archduke Franz Ferdinand, heir to the Austro-Hungarian throne, in Sarajevo, Serbia, on June 28, 1914. This seemingly isolated act triggered reactions across the complex network of alliances in Europe. By the end of August, Germany was at war with Russia and France and had invaded Belgium; Britain had declared war on Germany and won an initial naval battle; and Austria-Hungary was at war with Russia and had invaded Serbia. The Great War, the First World War, had begun.

By the end of September 1914, Germany had invaded through Belgium and into France—to within 30 miles of Paris and including the first battle of the Marne River. With both sides dug into close, opposite trenches, they created a Western Front that would remain virtually in place for four years and was the scene of extensive and horrific killing. Although both the French and especially the Germans made some attempts to attack and oust the opposition and gain ground, the four years would be characterized by mutual defensive attrition, with both sides (primarily the French and British, versus the Germans) suffering hundreds of thousands of casualties, with neither gaining a sustainable advantage. The Western Front remained largely in place, dominated by this trench warfare and associated artillery bombardment.

During the first half of 1915, the war in Europe was in full force. The Germans were bombing Britain from Zeppelins, the liner *Lusitania* was sunk by a German U-boat, and Italy declared war on Germany and Austria.

RESIGNATION

INCREASINGLY FRUSTRATED by President Woodrow Wilson's neutrality and reluctance to enter the war, and on duty in the Caribbean and feeling unable to personally contribute militarily to the Allied cause in Europe, Arthur Turner resigned his Marine Corps commission at the end of April 1915, "in order to permit my resuming civil life." As he was still aboard the *Nebraska*, Arthur tendered the resignation to MacArthur, as well as to Colonel John A. Lejeune, Assistant Marine Corps Commandant in Washington, and proposed that it take effect June 15. The effective date was moved up to June 1, however, to enable the Marine Corps to fill the resulting officer vacancy with an additional graduate of that year's class at the Naval Academy—reflecting the shortage of Marine Corps officers.

After docking at Philadelphia, Arthur was likely released from the Marines in advance of June 1 and immediately went to England and France, where he spent a good bit of the last half of 1915. He visited cousins and other relatives in Leeds and elsewhere in Yorkshire, perhaps to help out with their business there, or to gain help in dealing with his father's business in Pennsylvania. That initial trip as a civilian was a short one, as he left Liverpool on the ocean liner R.M.S. *Scandinavian* on June 15, heading to Quebec City and Montreal, Canada, and then overland on to Ottawa.

Exasperated with his country and his own indirect and distant role in the war in Europe, Arthur attempted to join the French infantry (owing to his and his father's affinity for France) but was turned down for not being a French citizen. He reputedly tried the same for the British Army and Navy, but was similarly unsuccessful. This probably was his primary reason for the 1915 trips to England and Europe, and perhaps his motivation for resigning from the Corps, after being 'cooped up' in the Gulf of Mexico and the Caribbean. A similar attempt in Canada may have been his reason for visiting Ottawa.

The *Scandinavian* was not loaded at Liverpool's main dock, because, in Arthur's words:

> "The *Mauretania* was using the dock to embark five thousand [British] troops for the Dardanelles. She looked magnificent with her four funnels and war paint and when she started down the river all the tugs let go their whistles and the crowd on shore set up a yell. She was convoyed by two torpedo destroyers."

This scene must have struck a particularly patriotic—and envious—chord with Arthur, the newly-resigned U.S. Marine watching a shipload of Brits go off to the war. Moreover, only six weeks before, the *Mauretania*'s sister ship, the *Lusitania*, had been sunk by German torpedoes just across the Irish Sea on its way to the same Liverpool docks, an event that turned the world irreversibly against the German war effort. The *Lusitania* was on Arthur's mind as, approaching Canada a few days later, he added in a note to his sister Edith that they "have seen nothing of the enemy's submarines."

In the same note to Edith, Arthur expresses his views about his fellow passengers on the *Scandinavian*:

> "The ship has only one cabin and steerage passengers. She is only carrying about one-quarter of the complement of passengers and the cabin lot are a very mixed assortment. There are several wounded Canadian Officers, on two months leave, a war writer, some nurses, a large number of slightly wounded Canadian soldiers, a fair number of business representatives, etc., on the passenger list. The service, meals, accommodations, etc., are superior to the American Liner *St. Louis*, but the passengers average a lower degree.

> They had one of those Seamen's Orphans Benefit Concerts last night and it was good in spots. As usual, I suppose."

Perhaps Arthur had gone from the U.S. to England on the *St. Louis*.

During this time, although he gave his correspondence address as 188 West River Street in Wilkes-Barre, his cable address was indicated as c/o John H. Turner, 17 High Ousegate, York, England—home of a prominent cousin of his father and one-time Lord High Sheriff of Yorkshire.

REJOINING

WHATEVER THE PURPOSE OF HIS TRAVELS, by late December 1915—only six months after resigning—Arthur Turner inquired about and then formally applied for reinstatement as a second lieutenant in the U.S. Marine Corps. Although the Marine commanding officers were quite keen on having him back, the process proved long and complicated. He was legally barred from reinstatement, because he was more than 27 years old, and a special act of Congress would be required to waive that restriction. Arthur managed to have a Pennsylvania Congressman sponsor a bill in the House of Representatives (H.R. 8277)—with a letter of support from the Secretary of the Navy to the House Chairman of Naval Affairs—which passed and was signed by President Wilson in August of 1916.

After that eight-month successful effort, however, he failed the physical exam in September, having been "found not physically qualified to perform the duties of a second lieutenant" for reasons unspecified, but probably due to his bad hearing and terrible uncorrected eyesight. However, newly-promoted General Lejeune overrode the disqualification in January 1917, and Arthur rejoined the Marines on April 30, 1917, some 16 months after his initial reinstatement application.

AMERICA MOBILIZES

M EANWHILE, THE WAR RAGED. On June 9, U.S. Secretary of State William Jennings Bryan, long opposed to President Wilson's policy of neutrality with Germany, resigned. In the 22 months between June 1915 and April 1917, the Western Front saw the costly and mostly futile battles at Verdun, Champagne and Loos, and the Somme. At Verdun alone, during the 10 months of German offensive and tenacious French defense beginning in February of 1916, some 360,000 French and 336,000 German soldiers were killed, with the front line moving only about five miles. Highly focused artillery added to the standoff in the trenches. And, the introduction of tanks and the use of airplanes for both bombing raids and dogfights, by both sides, were added to the fray.

Fighting along the Somme River began when British troops jumped their trenches on July 1, 1916, to charge embedded German positions. In that single day the British lost 20,000 dead or missing, with another 40,000 injured. Away from the Western Front, the Allies were routed at Gallipoli, the Germans were making marked progress against the Russians on the Eastern Front, and the largest naval battle of the war took place at Jutland (with no decisive result).

With Lenin and civil war erupting from the Russian revolution, beginning in March 1917, the prospect of a diminished German troop commitment to the Eastern Front created the potential release of nearly a million German soldiers for use in France. And, losses and mutiny among French forces during the year left Britain to bear the brunt of the Western Front campaign.

Although sympathy for the Allied countries fighting in Europe—especially Britain and France—was growing in the U.S., reluctance to consider entering the war remained strong too, including within the Wilson government. As a result, U.S. preparation for war was non-existent. As late as 1916, the country had fewer than 200,000 troops on active duty (although some 4.7 million would eventually serve during the next two years, two million of them in Europe).

AMERICA JOINS WW I

BY EARLY 1917, the rationale for the U.S. joining the war was finally gaining significant strength and acceptance in America. First, the plight of the Allies on the all-important Western Front was becoming desperate. With so many deaths from four years of battle (and sickness) and a depleted population from which to draw replacements, Britain and France were beginning to face troop shortages, especially for adult and trained men. And, as Germany continued to make progress in winning their war to the East against the Russians, the prospect of being able to redirect hundreds of thousands of German troops to assist in France added to Allied angst. And, finally, food and supply shortages abetted by German U-boat blockades around the Continent reduced the ability of the Allies to fight effectively indefinitely.

A second development triggering U.S. entry in the war was Germany's decision on February 1, 1917, to resume unrestricted submarine warfare. Until that time, starting shortly after the *Lusitania*'s sinking two years earlier, Germany had generally respected neutral countries' rights and avoided sinking their ships, despite significant amounts of food and supplies moving to the Allies in Europe. As a result of the new decision, the

U.S. broke off diplomatic relations with Germany on February 3. And, that same day, the U.S. ship *Housatonic*, on charter to Britain and carrying grain from Texas to England, was stopped and sunk by a German submarine near the British Scilly Isles, further boosting the strengthened pro-war and anti-Wilson party and public opinion in the U.S.

The third event prompting the U.S. to consider entering the war was public circulation in the U.S. of an intercepted telegram from German foreign secretary Zimmerman to the German ambassador in Mexico, proposing to establish a German-Mexican alliance if the U.S. were to declare war on Germany. The proposal specified that, upon victory, Texas, Arizona, and New Mexico would be annexed 'back' to Mexico. The telegram, intercepted by the British and passed to the Americans, was made public on March 1, inflaming the country.

Wilson had become convinced and could defer no longer, and the U.S. declared war on Germany on April 6, 1917. From that point forward, America's participation and the war itself were to last only 19 months. ✪

PART THREE

A Fateful Year in France

As the founding adjutant in the First Battalion,
Sixth Marine Regiment, Captain Turner is a leader in France
at the pivotal and savage Belleau Wood and Soissons battles,
losing a leg and ending his days on the battlefield,
while earning citations for bravery and gallantry.

ARTHUR TURNER REJOINED THE MARINES the same month the U.S. declared war—on April 30, 1917—following his nearly two-year stint as a civilian, and he must have been relieved by the declaration. He was commissioned a second lieutenant for the second time. The Navy recommendation stipulated that the reappointment would place his rank "at the foot of the list" of second lieutenants. Be that as it may, less than a month later, on May 22, he was promoted to first lieutenant, in view of his previous experience and excellent qualifications.

The formal presidential commission, ranking him a second lieutenant and signed by President Woodrow Wilson on June 12, 1917, arrived three weeks after he had been promoted to first lieutenant. The record was set straight in September, by including

Marine Corps commission, signed by President Wilson

Arthur in the list referenced by an entry into the Congressional Record: "The following-named first lieutenants to be first lieutenants in the Marine Corps for temporary service, from the 22nd day of May, 1917, to correct dates of present rank."

Of the 761 Marine Corps officers appointed between April 6 and the end of October 1917, Lieutenant Turner was the only former Marine officer reappointed.*

SOURCES OF USMC OFFICER APPOINTMENTS
April 6—October 31, 1917

Graduates of the Naval Academy	6
*Former officer of the Marine Corps	1
Former graduate of the Naval Academy	1
Warrant officers and paymaster's clerks of the Marine Corps	89
Meritorious noncommissioned officers of the Marine Corps	122
Reserve officers and national Naval Volunteers	36
Graduates of military colleges	284
Other civilians with prior military/naval experience/training	136
Other civilians passing the competitive July 10, 1917 exam	86

TOTAL APPOINTMENTS 761

It was no doubt rare, indeed perhaps unique, for a military officer to receive two separate Presidential commissions, at the same rank, four years apart.

ESTABLISHING THE AEF

P RESIDENT WILSON established the American Expeditionary Force (AEF) to build and lead all land forces deployed by the U.S. in the war, and on May 10, 1917, appointed General John J. 'Black Jack' Pershing to command the AEF. Pershing, 56 years old at the war's outbreak, was a West Point graduate with a long and distinguished record of service since the 1880's, including in the Spanish-American, Philippian-American, and Russo-Japanese wars. During the Mexican revolution, he had led an (unsuccessful) expedition to catch Poncho Villa in 1916-17, and years before, as a lieutenant, had taken part with then Colonel Theodore Roosevelt in the Battle of San Juan Hill in 1898. Pershing remained in command of the AEF for the duration of WWI.

From the outset, Pershing insisted that U.S. troops in Europe would remain under the command of U.S. officers—not be deployed merely as replacements (that is, 'fodder') for decimated French and British units—and would be adequately trained prior to their assignments to the front lines. Only a few thousand Army soldiers ('Doughboys') had been moved to France in May and June of 1917, but within a year, more than a million troops were stationed there, half of them making it to the front lines.

Ships were pressed into service as troop carriers, moving the newly-minted soldiers from New York, New Jersey, and Newport News, to the French harbors of Bordeaux, La Pallice, Saint Nazaire, and Brest, in order to connect with the French railway system. By year-end, 1917, Pershing had established training facilities in France near Verdun, and four AEF divisions had arrived, including the Second Division, consisting of regular Army troops and U.S. Marines.

The Marine component of the AEF was the Fourth Marine Brigade, of which the existing 5th Regiment was sent to France in July 1917 to await the Army. A brand new 6th Regiment was formed at Quantico, Virginia, initially with a "modest number of old-timers and mostly new recruits."

THE NEW 6TH MARINES

THE FIRST BATTALION SIXTH MARINES (referred to as the '1/6') was formed July 11, 1917. Although the battalion was to participate in many battles during the war, the one that is most remembered was to be the battle of Belleau Wood. The conduct of the Sixth and Fifth Marines there made the entire Corps legendary.

Lieutenant Arthur Turner, perhaps qualifying as an 'old-timer' at age 29 and with experience in the Caribbean, was ordered to the Marine base at Quantico, and assisted in founding that to-be-famous 6th Marines Regiment. Promoted again, to Captain (effective May 23—yes, the day after his 1st Lieutenant appointment), he was the first Executive Officer, or adjutant,

**1st Battalion,
6th Regiment
Marines Insignia**

of the 6th Regiment's 1st Battalion, which was formed and activated on July 11, 1917. During the next two months, he also was the first Company Commander of, in turn, the "B" and "D" companies, as mostly newly-recruited men arrived to form those units. The role of these light infantry battalions was to "locate, close with and destroy the enemy by fire and maneuver," and the battalion's mottos were—and remain to this day—"Ready to Fight since 1917" and "1/6 HARD." The 1/6 had been assigned to the Fourth Brigade, Second Army Division of the AEF.

MARRIAGE

THREE MONTHS into his second Marine Corps stint, based at Quantico, and with the U.S. now fully engaged in the war, Arthur married Dorothy H. Innes of a prominent Wilkes-Barre family on September 1, 1917, in Philadelphia. They had known each other for some time, probably since childhood, as Dorothy's family lived on Mallery Place, just around the corner from the Turner household on West River Street. Dorothy was born May 7, 1883 and so was four years older than Chuie. Her maternal grandmother was a descendent of the Reverend Michael Enterline, a Lutheran minister who came to the English colonies from Holland in 1765 and established the Lutheran Church in America. As far as we know, however, Dorothy (or 'Dot' to some, but not to Arthur) had no qualms attending Episcopal Churches for most of her life.

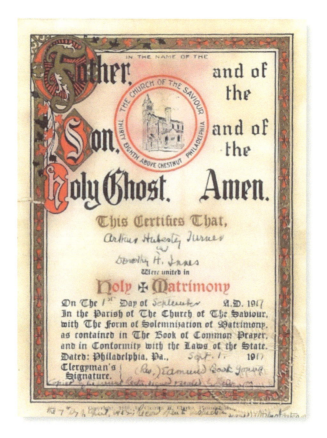

Arthur and Dorothy's Marriage Certificate, September 1, 1917

Because Arthur was in Philadelphia on only a short leave from Quantico, there was no honeymoon trip for the newlyweds. Expecting Arthur to remain at Quantico for at least two more months, they moved into an apartment in Fredericksburg, Virginia, and were "very pleasantly located" there, with an easy daily commute to Quantico for Arthur. However, Arthur's orders to "shove off" came earlier than expected—after only a single week in the apartment.

FRANCE AT LAST

D ESPITE DELAYS in constructing new barracks at Quantico and a shortage of trained officers, three quarters of the regiment's enlisted men were in place there by mid-August. And, by early September, four companies had been organized into the First Battalion, under the command of Major John A. Hughes, nicknamed 'Johnny the Hard.' The First Battalion companies were the 74th, 75th, 76th, and 95th. Without waiting for the rest of the regiment to be filled out, they were scheduled to leave on September 16.

Major Hughes, his adjutant Captain Turner, and the 1/6 left Quantico by train early on Sunday September 16, 1917, for Philadelphia, headed for France. The post band played in the rain, "and as the trains pulled away from the station the battalion was given a rousing cheer" by those remaining at the base.

The train arrived at Philadelphia at about six in the evening that same day. Having been told that the ship would probably leave Philadelphia on Thursday, Dorothy and a girlfriend traveled to Philadelphia Sunday morning and rented a small apartment there for a few days (at the Colonial at 11th and Spruce streets; $25 per week, including meals). But, Arthur received word that the Marines would leave on the transport ship U.S.S. *Henderson* at 8:00 the next morning and that the ship would be stocked in New York, rather than Philadelphia, before crossing the Atlantic. Captain Turner—as adjutant—frantically worked to get the more than 1,000 Marine "boobs" settled and fed aboard the ship, and Dorothy came down to the League Island dock and stayed in Arthur's office there while he worked until 11:30 that night. They then took a taxi to the apartment, but got up at five on Monday morning, taking a taxi back to the ship, where they had breakfast in the Marine Officers' Mess Room, before saying good bye before the *Henderson* shoved off.

In a letter to his sister Edith, written aboard the *Henderson* at sea, Arthur reflected on that moment:

> "It was awfully hard to leave her, especially since we were both prepared for at least four or five days at Phila. Dorothy has certainly acted as only the bravest and finest act since we have been married. She has been content to do anything or go anywhere I ask and at any time and always happy and cheerful about it. I think I picked a prize. She has tried to help me in everything and got along beautifully with all the service people in Fredericksburg. I can't say enough for her."

He closed his letter asking Edith to give her three young children "some good kisses from 'Chuie' and with love to all the family, your devoted brother, Arthur."

Docking in New York on Monday evening, the *Henderson* spent the next five days taking on supplies, and also waiting until the convoy was formed, with the ship's crew and soldier passengers—including Arthur—remaining on board and unable to go

The U.S.S. *Henderson*, carrying troops and supplies
from New York to St. Nazaire, France, in late 1917.

ashore. Perhaps unknown to Arthur, Dorothy had continued on
from Philadelphia to New York to see him off, staying in a hotel
overlooking the harbor, with the troop ship in sight, and waiting day after day to waive good-by again. When she awoke on
Monday morning, the ship was gone, having sailed on Sunday
the 23rd, at 10:30 PM.

This was one of nine voyages the four-month-old *Henderson*
made ferrying troops and supplies to France, across the subma-
rine-infested Atlantic. She had space for 1,500 men and 24 mules.

The *Henderson* and its military cargo survived an uneventful, even dull, 12-day crossing. Captain Turner was one of 27 Marine Corps officers to make the voyage, along with the Battalion's 1,045 enlisted men and a complement of medical staff and chaplains. The men were in the hold, where they slept on the deck, except for a few lucky ones with hammocks. The constant swells striking the ship, combined with the tight quarters and lack of air in the hold, kept many men seasick throughout the trip.

The officers had it better—along with the nurses aboard—with fresh air bunks to sleep in on the promenade deck, and better meals that could be served in their rooms if they wished. In the continuously rough sea, however, many of the officers also suffered bouts of seasickness.

An historical fiction short story based in some detail on Captain Turner by author Thomas Boyd—who knew him and was with him in the 1/6—revealed his bent for cigars aboard the *Henderson*, citing him as "puffing at some of those long thin stogies which it was his habit to smoke incessantly."

At last, Arthur had achieved his ambition to reach France and was to see action.

The first three months in France, however, were spent attending First Army Corps Schools in the village of Gondrecourt, 435 miles and well past Paris to the east, for a month of training, and then returning to St. Nazaire for another seven weeks of Marine training and various non-combat duties. These included camp guard duty, longshoremen's work at the docks, and building a dam and a variety of other structures and buildings, as the camp expanded near the port.

Captain Turner's AEF Identity Card, No. 238

In December, Quantico sent a request to St. Nazaire, that Arthur and three other Marine Corps officers be notified that each had left their Quantico barracks "inadvertently overlooking" that they owed money for August mess bills, in amounts ranging from 40 cents to $3. Arthur, then 10 weeks in France, owed $1.80.

On January 6, 1918, the First Battalion left St. Nazaire again by train, traveling for nearly three days and some 490 miles east to Champigneulles in the Vosges region near Nancy. This location was the designated Marine training area, about 60 miles north of the Sixth Marine Regiment headquarters at Blevaincourt. By the end of January, the First Battalion had encamped there along with the Third Battalion, and they were joined soon after by the Second Battalion.

These pictures of Captain Turner in late 1917 reveal some horsemanship, as well as the round, felt 'field hat' that was the combat hat of choice until the British convinced and provided the Americans with the hard, 'wash-bowl' helmets used thenceforth.

About six weeks of grueling training followed, to mid-March. With a backdrop of severe weather, the program included "hikes, close order drill, bayonet practice, rifle and grenade throwing, trench storming, taking strong points and gas attacks."

As the war wore on and casualties mounted, future Marine replacements were to receive little or no training in France, as most of them were hurried into the fighting shortly upon arrival from the U.S.

FRONT LINE ACTION

L ATE ON MARCH 17, the First Battalion left by train for the front lines, detraining early on March 18 at Lemmes (about 50 miles northwest), and then immediately marching nine miles east to Sommedieue, and taking up a reserve position behind the French 10th Army Corps, just behind the front line.

Pershing's intensive training program included front line trench action to acclimate the new U.S. Army and Marine Corps men to their new and challenging front line roles. This 'live' training was to be carried out in areas along the front that were relatively calm or at least stable, and Turner's baptism at the front near Sommedieue was one such experience.

For two months—from March 17 to May 14—Major Hughes and his 1/6 battalion served two two-week periods as the Front Line Battalion, including 19 days in the Cote des Hures Sector, and 14 days near Haudiomont. The 1/6 shuttled between its camp and the nearby lines of trenches, between the River Meuse and the north-south oriented trenches.

After nearly a month of relative quiet, with some German shelling attacks and limited French and American patrols, the Germans launched a deadly gas attack early the morning of April 12, catching most of the officers and men without their gas masks. All the officers and 220 men were debilitated by the gas, with 40 dying later from the attack. The gas attacks continued for the rest of the month, with 1/6 adjutant Arthur Turner sending a message to 6th Regiment commander Colonel Albertus Catlin on the evening of April 25: "6:30 tonight one gas shell fell just off right front line. Also more gas shells falling on hill to right of our front line." Although Arthur believed he had been

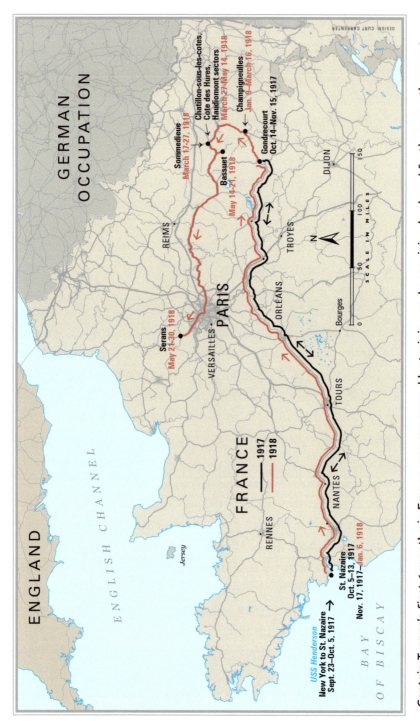

Captain Turner's first 6 months in France was consumed by training and organizing back and forth across the country, followed by another 2 months of front line action and support around Sommedieue, resting at Serans at the end of May.

in contact with mustard gas, he did not seem affected at the time and certainly had no lasting effects.

Five days later, the 1/6 had returned to its nearby control point, P.C. Bordeaux.

During April and the first half of May, the battalion also played reserve and support roles at Camps Ronde Fontaine, Massa, and Rozelliere. A headquarters had been set up at Camp Boues, and various 'posts of command' were established at the regiment and battalion levels.

With two months of live front line experience behind him, Captain Turner and the 1/6 moved some 50 miles west for a week of rest at the town of Bassuet, and then travelled farther west for an additional week at Serans, on the River Oise, west of Paris.

GERMAN GAINS HALTED

WHILE THE 1/6 was completing its training and baptismal trench warfare, the spring of 1918 marked a German attempt at a knockout blow to the Allies on the Western Front. In March, with the imminent arrival of hundreds of U.S. troops in France, German General Ludendorff began transferring dozens of his divisions from the Russian Eastern Front and successfully gained territory attacking to the west of Reims and marching down the Marne valley towards Paris. After four years of deadlock on the Front, Germany launched its last, desperate Spring Offensive.

By the end of May, Allied forces in France seemed near defeat as the Germans steadily drove toward Paris, annihilating the British 5th Army. The long Chemin des Dames ridge had been

® 11368

The 1/6 officers at P.C. Bordeaux on April 30, 1918, exactly a year after Captain Turner rejoined the Marines. Left to right: Captain O.R. Cauldwell, Captain A.H. Turner, Lieutenant Carlton Burr, Major R.E. Adams, and Interpreter Brewster Reamey. Adams was transitioning off as Battalion commander, succeeded until June 8 by Major Maurice Shearer. Captain Turner remained the 1/6 adjutant.

regarded as impregnable, but the Germans passed it apparently without the slightest difficulty, and then overtook the town of Soissons and many others, reaching the town of Lucy-le-Bocage, less than 50 miles from Paris. The Germans were advancing along a forty-mile front and on May 28th had reached past the River Aisne, with the French and British steadily falling back. This was the great German Spring Offensive, or "Victory Drive," and each day registered a new Allied defeat. The papers from day to day were chronicling wonderful enemy successes, and the anxiety among the Allies was indescribable. An estimated one million French residents fled Paris, lest they be overrun by the invading Germans.

On May 29th, however, under great headlines announcing a German gain of ten miles in which the Germans had taken twenty-five thousand prisoners and crossed two rivers, had captured Soissons, and were threatening Rheims, there appeared in American papers "a quiet little dispatch" from General Pershing. It read: "This morning in Picardy our troops attacked on a front of one and one-fourth miles, advanced our lines, and captured the village of Cantigny. We took two hundred prisoners, and inflicted on the enemy severe losses in killed and wounded. Our casualties were relatively small. Hostile counter-attacks broke down under our fire."

This Allied attack at Cantigny was the first American offensive, and the Allies' first distinct advance. With an hour of artillery preparation, the infantry followed with clock-like precision, fierce hand-to-hand fighting ensued, and the Americans hurled hand grenades like baseballs into the tunnels and caves. On May 30th, General Pershing announced there would be the complete repulse of further enemy attacks from the new American positions near Cantigny.

After the Cantigny battle, American Second Division troops were hurried to the front at a gap in the French line east of Meaux, across the Paris-Metz road near Montreuil-aux-Lions. This stopped the German advance on Paris, and the spot was as far west as the Germans would come.

The ensuing Allied push to stop and then turn back the German lines on the Western Front proved the War's turning point and began the rapid march to the War's end, with the 1/6 in the forefront. Captain Turner remained adjutant, or Executive Officer, of the 1st Battalion "when they all made history at Belleau Wood and Soissons."

The fighting at and around Belleau Wood in June stopped the Germans and put an end to their expansion into Allied territory. And, the subsequent Allied offensive battles around Soissons, lasting about two weeks in July, began the final rout of the German forces.

BELLEAU WOOD

D URING THE MONTH-LONG June Battle of Belleau Wood, the Marines played the lead role in stopping the German advance and pushing them back.

> "Fighting with rifles and bayonets, the U.S. troops advanced against well-emplaced German machine gun positions and heavy artillery fire and suffered heavy losses. Fighting day and night without relief, without sleep, often without water, and for days without hot rations, the Marines met and defeated the best divisions that Germany could muster. The heroism and doggedness were unparalleled. Time after time officers seeing

their lines cut to pieces, seeing their men so dog tired that they even fell asleep under shellfire, hearing their wounded calling for the water they were unable to supply, seeing men fight on after they had been wounded and until they dropped unconscious; time after time officers seeing these things, believing that the very limit of human endurance had been reached, would send back messages to their post command that their men were exhausted. But, told that their line must be held and advanced, without water, food, rest, they went forward."

Some companies lost every officer, with troop complements decimated.

Captain Turner and his battalion left Serans late on May 30, traveling overnight by bus, and arrived at 6:00 A M at Montreuil-aux-Lions, 80 miles east. About 1:00 P M, after eating "anything and everything that wasn't nailed down," they continued on, marching the remaining five miles northward, off the highway to just north of Lucy-le-Bocage, as German shells began falling in a nearby field. They continued to extend their line northward on the road to Torcy, sheltering in the St. Martin woods, and being in place by 7:30 P M on June 1.

Meanwhile, back in the States, the Marine Corps Major General Commandant George Barnett on that same day received a letter from Arthur's father, indicating that Arthur had requested a box of cigars and inquiring as to how he might get it to him, because an endorsement from "a ranking officer" was required. In his request, Charles Turner pointed out that "the quality cigars on that side are far different from what we have here." Barnett responded that if Arthur's father would send him the cigars, he would make sure someone took them to Arthur in France. It is

Headquarters U. S. Marine Corps,

Washington, June 5, 1918.

My dear Mr. Turner:

      I am in receipt of your letter of
the 1st instant, relative to your desire to send some
cigars to your son, Captain Arthur H. Turner, now
serving with the American Expeditionary Forces in
France, and in reply permit me to inform you that if
you will send the cigars here to these Headquarters,
I will be very glad to see to it that they are carried over by some officer in the next over-seas con-
tingent, and delivered to Captain Turner.

      Assuring you that it is a pleasure to be of this
little service,

        Very cordially,

           George Barnett

        Major General Commandant.

Mr. C. S. Turner,
    44 South Pennsylvania Ave.,
    Wilkes-Barre, Pa.

The personal letter from the Commandant of the United States
Marine Corps in Washington to Arthur's father Charles,
volunteering to personally see that a box of cigars
would be forwarded to Captain Turner in France—
as the Battle of Belleau Wood was gearing up.

unknown if the cigars got through, before Arthur left France in September.

The vanguard of the German advance reached and occupied Belleau Wood during June 2 and 3, but a failed German assault at Les Mares Farm on June 4 defined the high water mark of the German offensive and the closest they got to Paris during the war. The 1/6 served as the left flank Front Line Battalion on June 2 repulsing the German infantry attack; held its ground the next day; and remained on the Front Line at Mares Farm on June fourth.

Also on the fourth, a three-man Marine patrol located enemy forces at Torcy and, hiding there for more than an hour with the sounds of German voices close by, returned with definite intelligence that was of great value in framing the Allied attack a few days later.

THE ORDER TO ATTACK

ON JUNE 5, the French commander ordered the U.S. Army Second Division to take back Belleau Wood, and the main assault fell to the Fourth Marine Brigade, who were near the Wood. The 1st Battalion 6th Regiment moved to a reserve position for the French Army at La Platriere Farm for three days, and then as Brigade reserve to the woods near Lucy.

A French reconnaissance pilot had reported Belleau Wood to be free of German occupants. But, the German Army had in fact taken the entire Wood and turned it into a bastion. American troops were immediately consumed with silencing enemy machine gun nests, fending off and capturing charging German soldiers, and mounting bayonet charges of their own.

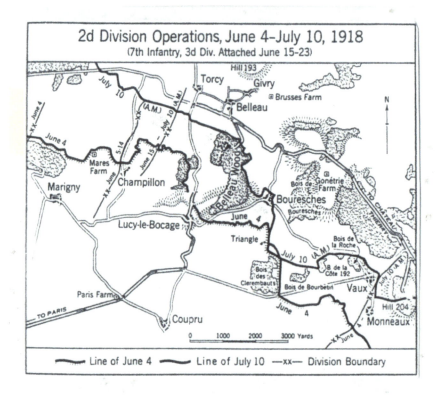

The Belleau Wood vicinity, with Mares Farm to the west, Torcy to the north, Lucy-le-Bocage to the south, and Bouresches to the east. The heavy black lines indicate the original Allied positions on June 4, 1918, and the progress made by July 10. Generally, the 5th Marines occupied the area to the left of Belleau Wood, and the 6th Marines to the right.

Starting at 5:00 AM on June 6, the 1st/5 captured Hill 142, west of the Wood, to support an attack that the 3/5 and 3/6 carried out on the Wood 12 hours later as a frontal assault from the south and west, with the 2/6 eventually taking the village of Bouresches to the east of the Wood.

The attack went grimly. Crossing a wheat field where they were exposed to machine gun fire, Gunnery Sargent Dan Daly famously urged his men on, "Come on ya sons-of-bitches, ya want to live forever?" The attack succeeded in taking only a small corner of the Wood, and with the struggle to get into the southern edge of the woods, the 2/6 in reserve near Triangle Farm was ordered to take Bouresches. A few lead Marines got into the village, but retaining it was a struggle due to the Marine flanks being wide-open fields, with any attempted reinforcements receiving heavy German fire.

But, personal bravery kept the Marines at Bouresches supplied. That night, with word that Bouresches had been taken by a handful of Marines but was in desperate need of rations and ammunition, three volunteers drove a truck loaded with the vital supplies over a shell-torn dirt road, under the light of flares and star shells, and through heavy fire. The same evening, a 21-year-old lieutenant captured seventeen Germans and two machine guns with his platoon in a bayonet charge. And, another lieutenant directed artillery fire during part of the attack on the Wood, from a tree where he had observation of the German lines, backed up with the knowledge he had gained on his ground patrol.

On this day, June 6, 1918, the Marine Brigade suffered the worst single day's casualties in USMC history to that point, with 31 officers and 1,056 men killed or wounded—perhaps exceeding, collectively, the total of all previous casualties in the Marine Corps' entire history.

THE 1/6 JOINS THE FRONT LINE

FROM JUNE 6 THROUGH 9, the 1/6 was in reserve status—the first three days at La Platriere farm, and June 9 in the woods next to Lucy-le-Bocage. On the battlefield, in the 24 hours from noon on June 8 to noon on June 9, almost 7,000 German

This print portrays Marines grappling with the enemy in hand-to-hand combat on June 6 at Belleau Wood. There are fewer trenches and greater reliance on artillery barrages, but still the horror of bayonets and face-to-face, to-the-death fighting.

artillery shells fell, including a significant number of gas shells.

Young replacements were told, "Com on, now; lemme hear you 'What do we wash our bay 'nets in?—German blood—Aw sing out like you meant it, you dam' replacements! I'll swear, it's a shame to feed animals like you to the Germans."

And, preparing for gas attacks: "Gas-mask drill—Take more than five seconds, an' your Maw gets a Gold Star!"

Regrouping and a new American assault had failed to gain ground the previous three days, but at 4:30 A M on June 10, heavy American artillery began paving the way for the next attack to capture Belleau Wood. Marine units deep in the woods were

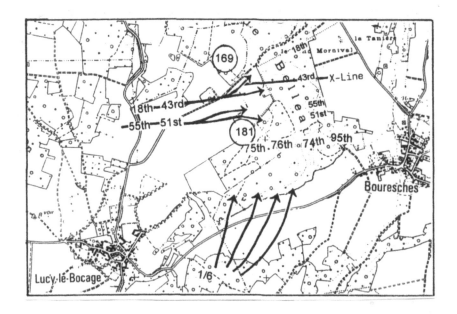

The four companies of the 1/6 Marines (75th, 76th, 74th, 95th) advanced from below the Lucy-Bouresches road on June 10 to occupy the southern part of Belleau Wood. On the following day, Lieutenant Colonel Wise led his 2/5 Marines into the northern part of the Wood, but it would be three more weeks before the Germans were entirely cleared out.

ordered to withdraw to the south edge of the trees to avoid the Allied shelling.

The all-out assault—lead by the 1/6—succeeded in taking the southern two thirds of the Wood on June 11, and the remaining third to the north was broken through on the 12th. On June 11, the official statement of the French War Office declared: "South of the Ourcq River the American troops this morning brilliantly captured Belleau Wood, and took three hundred prisoners."

After two weeks of these intense battles, a captured German officer with his dying breath warned of a fresh division of Germans that was about to be thrown into battle to wrest from the Marines that part of the Wood they had gained. The Marines straightened their lines and prepared for the imminent attack. On the 13th, the major German counterattack began at 2:00 AM, hurling its forces against both the town of Bouresches and the Bois de Belleau. But the depleted Marine lines held. With their backs to the trees and boulders of the Wood, and with their sole shelter the scattered ruins of Bouresches, the thinning lines of the Marines repelled the attack and crushed the new German division. Although the Americans retained control of Bouresches and their part of the Wood, they also suffered heavy casualties, including from intense gas attacks.

On June 17, the remaining 1/6 leaders (12 officers, including two replace-ments), and the greatly depleted battalion complement of men were on the way to a rest camp at Nanteuil-sur-Marnce, about nine miles to the south of the Wood, near Montreuil-aux-Lions. Then Battalion commander Major Franklin Garrett is at the right of the front group, Captain Turner third from right. The caption for the AEF photo is "Heroes of Bois de Belleau."

And so it had gone: day after day, night after night, with similar messages travelling from the positions to the post command: "Losses heavy. Difficult to get runners through. Some have never returned. Morale excellent, but troops about all in. Men exhausted." The 1/6 spent the seven days from June 17 to June 25 regrouping and resting as Battalion Reserve at Nanteuil and then as Brigade Reserve in woods east of Montreuil.

By June 24th, the day-by-day advancement at the Front was capped by a tremendous barrage, which tore the woods to pieces, but still required remaining machine gun nests to be removed by the American method of rush and bayonet. The 1/6 spent the subsequent 10 days again as the Front Line Battalion clearing the Wood. This was completed on July 5, when the last remaining Marines, with the feeling of work well done, were relieved by Army replacements.

"Finally it was taken, by inches."

BUILDING REPUTATIONS

THE BATTLE was such a hard-won success that General Pershing—an Army man and initially no great admirer of the Marines—was to declare: "The deadliest weapon in the world is a Marine and his rifle!" and "the Battle of Belleau Wood was for the U.S. the biggest battle since Appomattox and the most considerable engagement American troops had ever had with a foreign enemy."

French General Degoutte issued an order on June 30 as follows: "In view of the brilliant conduct of the 4th Brigade of the 2nd U.S. Division, which in a spirited fight took Bouresches and the important strong point of Bois de Belleau, stubbornly defended by a large enemy force, the General Commanding the VI Army orders that henceforth, in all official papers, the Bois de Belleau shall be named Bois de la Brigade de Marine." Official French maps were modified accordingly, and this tribute demonstrates the deep effect that the retaking of the Wood and nearby positions had on the feelings of the French and the morale of the Allies.

> "While Hughes was very much in control of his battalion during this period, his adjutant, Captain Turner, was at all times in the forefront of operations against the enemy. Under all types of hazards and shelling, both gas and shrapnel, Turner exerted control over the many facets of the battalion while in action at Belleau Wood, especially during the period June 10 to 13."

Although most regimental and inter-battalion dispatches and communications on the Western front were authored by the battalion commander at the time, Turner's intelligence gathering and coordination were 'written all over' those reports. Under terrific shell fire and days of constant combatant movement, the ensuring of liaison and the execution of orders—among the companies of 1/6, and among the other Marine units and with the Army and French commands—was carried out under Captain Turner's personal supervision, contributing materially to the success of the attack against the strong and entrenched enemy.

For his participation in the fighting in and around Belleau Wood from Thursday, June 6th to Thursday the 13th, Captain Turner was awarded the French Croix de Guerre with Gilt Star for gallantry. A Marine Corps cable dispatch reported that Captain Turner had displayed "unusual courage in the face of the enemy," during the fighting in the Bois de Belleau. "Captain Turner, in the face of ter-

This picture shows Belleau Wood after the German, French, and American artillery had made it look this way. The view is what the Marines saw as they tried to take what was left of it.

rific shellfire, personally maintained connections in the wood... thus insuring the concentration of the various units."

The citation from the French government said, "He displayed coolness, courage and determination during all the operations at the Belleau Wood from June 10-13, 1918. He kept up the communications under a terrible artillery fire thus contributing to the success of the attack."

La Croix de Guerre awards, inaugurated by the French in April 1915, were bestowed on Americans with a lavish hand during the war, to those soldiers whose deeds were considered of extraordinary merit, as recommended by their captains. Levels of superior officers could add a bronze palm leaf or gold or bronze star to the ribbon, and Arthur's gold star indicated recognition at the Corps level.

Croix de Guerre with Gilt Star, Silver Star

Captain Turner also received the American Silver Star Medal, cited by the A E F Commanding General for gallantry in action at Belleau Wood. The Silver Star is the third highest personal decoration for valor in combat, exceeded only by the Distinguished Service Cross and the Medal of Honor.

Many years later, Arthur learned that his Regimental Commander at Belleau Wood, Colonel Harry Lee, had in June of 1918 formally recommended him for the Distinguished Service Cross (D S C), but the recommendation was "disapproved" two months later.

The Marine nickname Devil Dogs emanated from Belleau Wood, where official German reports referred to the Marines as "Teufel Hunden." The nickname arose when Marines were ordered to take a hill occupied by German forces, while wearing gas masks as a precaution against German mustard gas. From the Germans' vantage point, they witnessed a pack of tenacious, sweating, growling figures wearing gas masks, with bloodshot eyes and mouth foam seeping from the sides, advancing up the hill, sometimes on all fours, killing everything in their way. As the legend goes, the German soldiers began to yell that they were being attacked by "dogs from hell."

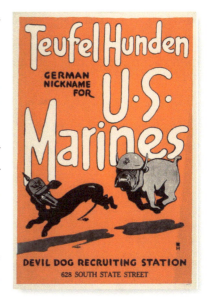

Devil Dog
recruiting poster.

In the three weeks in June, the American 2nd Division had stopped the advancing German army for good, enabling the Allies to reoccupy Hill 142, Belleau Wood, and the towns of Bouresches and Vaux. But, these accomplishments had a casualty cost of 170 officers and 8,739 men, of whom 112 officers and 4,598 men were Marines. In the weeks that followed, incoming replacements made up most of the numbers, but not the level of experience.

On July 2, a detail of Marines—the ones with the cleanest uniforms—was sent to Paris for a 4th of July parade, and they were hailed as the "saviours of Paris."

After being finally relieved by parts of the Army 26th Division on July 5 and 6, Arthur and the Marines moved to the rear of the lines, near Montreuil-aux-Lions and Nanteuil-ser-Marne. Here, they established a provisional Line of Defense and remained until mid-July. Captain Turner and the 1/6 spent three days in reserve in the woods south of Bezu-le-Guery, south of Montreuil. Although for only a short time, they were able to rest, refit, clean up, get some good chow, and swim in the River Marne. They then spent eight days in the second line trenches between Bezu-le-Guery and Montreuil.

SOISSONS

AFTER DINNER ON JULY 16, the entire Second Division, including the 6th Marines, departed Montreuil, making their way about 25 miles north until being dropped off in a field near the town of Pierrefonds about noon on the 17th. (There were few maps available, the 6th Marines receiving only a single copy.) From there they marched the remaining 12 miles to the Foret de Retz, just east of Villers-Cotterets and 22 miles from the town of Soissons. "They will remember the march to the Soissons battle, through the dark and the rain...."

They were positioning to attack the following morning—the first major offensive with French Marshal Foch in charge of the grand forces. Early that morning, newly-promoted Major General James Harbord, their Division Commander, directly gave Captain Turner the orders to have the 1st Battalion, 6th Marines, move to its position for what was to become the Soissons offensive on July 18 and 19. The 6th Marines moved up to leapfrog the decimated Second Division Army infantry units, as well as the 5th Marines.

Very early on July 18, the 5th Marines and the 23rd Army Regiment commenced the Grand Attack and advanced at intervals taking La Verte-Feuille Farm and Beaurepaire Farm, driving the Germans back about 10 miles. At about 8:00 AM, they were approaching the village of Vierzy. They suffered heavy casualties, but captured Vierzy by day's end. Although the 6th Regiment had had a tough time getting to the assignment, and were in a support position, they too participated actively on the afternoon of July 18. Late in the day, Brigade headquarters was moved to a cave in Vierzy.

"The following day—July 19—was just the 6th Marines and no one else, and they paid an awful price for the 'honor.' Their objective was to sever the great Soissons-Chateau-Thierry road, against more and fresher German defenders brought up overnight. With Major John Hughes recently back from hospital treatment of his Belleau Wood gassing and now again in command of the 1/6, that Battalion was on the right flank, with 2/6 on the left and 3/6 in the support line. At 7:30 that morning, the 1/6 established their lines just outside Vierzy, then went forward, through the town, and up the ravine to the level plain, with 28 French tanks following, and settled in an open wheat field, somewhat exposed to enemy artillery and machine gun fire.

Allied artillery had already fired a rolling barrage at 6:30 AM, so when the 6th was to jump off at 8:30 in and beyond Vierzy, there was no rolling barrage for them. Worse, the Germans were ready. The only artillery fire the Marines witnessed was incoming and dropping on them. The regiment had to cross more than two miles of open and partially-wooded field to their target city of Tigny. Most would not make it, and Hughes' 1/6 was 'badly handled' and 'reduced to shreds.'"

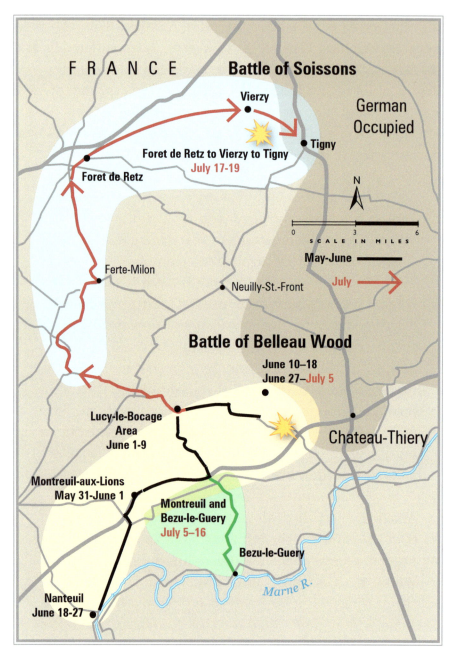

F R A N C E   **Battle of Soissons**

Vierzy

German Occupied

Tigny

Foret de Retz to Vierzy to Tigny
July 17-19

Foret de Retz

N

0   3   6
SCALE IN MILES

May-June ——

July ⟶

Ferte-Milon

Neuilly-St.-Front

Battle of Belleau Wood

June 10–18
June 27–July 5

Lucy-le-Bocage Area
June 1-9

Chateau-Thiery

Montreuil-aux-Lions
May 31-June 1

Montreuil and Bezu-le-Guery
July 5–16

Bezu-le-Guery

Marne R.

Nanteuil
June 18-27

Captain Turner spent the month of June, 1918 preparing for battle and taking Belleau Wood, and then moved 25 miles to the north, preparing to engage and overtake the Germans at the front toward Soissons.

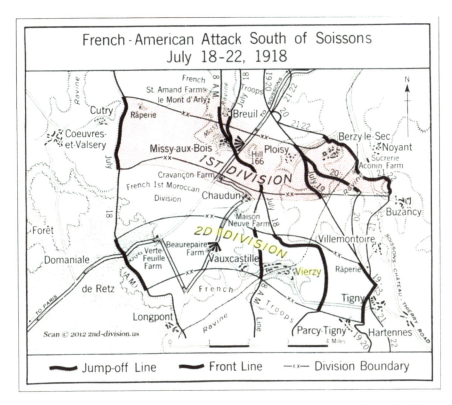

The area south of the town of Soissons, where the 1st American Division to the north, and the 2nd American Division to the south, launched major assaults on the enemy, from July 18 to 22, 1918. The 1/6 Marines joined the movement from Beaurepaire Farm on the 18th and on the 19th led the push from Vierzy toward Tigny.

Beginning the forward attack about 8:15 A M on July 19, they moved forward rapidly, despite the artillery and ground-fire onslaught and continuing losses, gaining approximately two miles and reaching about 300 yards short of Tigny.

One Marine in the 3rd Battalion that day, John Thomason, in his book *Fix Bayonets!*, portrays the horror of the incoming artillery:

"There may be shells, shrapnel, and H.E., [High Explosives] searching the ground, one can hear them coming. 'Is it gonna hit me—is it gonna hit me, O Lawd—Christ! that was close!' Presently pain, in recurring waves. Pride may lock a man's lips awhile . . . left long enough, most men break, and no blame to them. A hundred brave dead, lying where the guns cut them down, are not so pitiful as one poor wailing fellow in a dressing-station . . . ."

Another observation as the morning progressed:

"We lay there in these shallow trenches with the Boche artillery pounding the life out of us, with the sun roasting us, with gas choking us, and with the Boche airplanes swooping down and firing machine guns into us." The German artillery, in particular, "was so great that it seemed like a black curtain."

And a description of the advance of Hughes and Turner's 1/6:

"The French tanks, dispersed at fifty-yard intervals among the infantry, drew the bulk of artillery fire coming from guns only four thousand yards away as the waves of Marines passed through the forward foxholes of the (departed) 23rd Infantry. The doughboys urged the Marines to take cover, but the lines of men pressed forward.... they decided they could go no farther when the last tank in the area exploded from a direct hit. Almost immediately, the remnants of the company fell into the thin concealment of the wheat field."

**The 6th Regiment advancing across a field
between Vierzy and Tigny on July 19.**

Recalled another participant:

"In 10 minutes we had ten men blown to pieces and twenty wounded within fifty yards of us.....The machine gun fire encountered before the town of Bouresches was bad but the fire now is a thousand times worse.... It is like a hailstorm....My body is bent forward as though forcing myself through a heavy rain....There are crooked little paths through the wheat....at the end of each little path lies a dead soldier. Sergeant McFadden has the group next to me on the left...he is leading. All of a sudden he swerves around, facing our group. He has a terrified, surprised look of agony on his face.... His hands clutch the air one moment, then they wrap themselves about his stomach....His teeth gnash....Biting the air, he staggers back and falls."

CAPTAIN TURNER TAKEN OUT

B Y 10:00 A M, the 1/6 had made it to about 300 yards in front of Tigny, but was held up there by the rain of artillery shelling. About that time, an incoming high-explosive ('HE') artillery shell killed or wounded all but one of the staff officers of the 1/6, one of the wounded being Captain Arthur Turner. The shell—a 110-pound high energy shell from a German Minenwerfer 'mine thrower' cannon—landed and exploded two men down the line from Turner. The blast knocked down the man closest to it and killed the Marine next to Turner. A piece of hot, sharp shrapnel clipped off the heel and back of Turner's left foot, basically shattering it.

Author Boyd portrays Turner sitting on the ground in the wheat field, bleeding and unable to stand, and retrieving from his pocket and lighting up "one of those long black stogies which he buys in job lots." Presumably, General Barnett's delivery from Arthur's father had not yet reached him.

The Captain was removed to the regimental dressing station in a large cave, which was several kilometers away, probably at either brigade headquarters at Vierzy or at Beaurepaire Farm, which was serving as an advanced aid station. There, he steadfastly refused to be treated in advance of a great number of wounded men. He had lost his foot, and "the knowledge that he was out of the game, and that other men could be returned for duty if operated on ahead of him, held him to his purpose."

Behind that field station was a huge pile of human limbs—blown off by incoming shells and cast off from immediate amputations. The image of that pile haunted Captain Turner and gave him nightmares for years afterward.

A Minenwerfer H.E. 17, used to propel high-explosive 'bombs' onto Allied trenches, tanks, and troops as they moved toward the village of Tigny on July 19, 1918.

Describing the environment on July 19, Hughes sent the following message to (Regiment Commander) Colonel Lee at 10:15 that morning:

"P.C/ 1 kilometer due east of TIGNY. My Bn. Held up 300 yards W. of TIGNY. No troops on right. None on left. Tanks all out of action. Request immediate reinforcements. Dr. Mack only Dr. with me. Need doctors and some means to evacuate badly wounded. Request counter battery work at once. Remnants of Bn. Clear of TIGNY to west. Have about 200 men left. Lt. Cates 96th Co. reports 20 survivors."

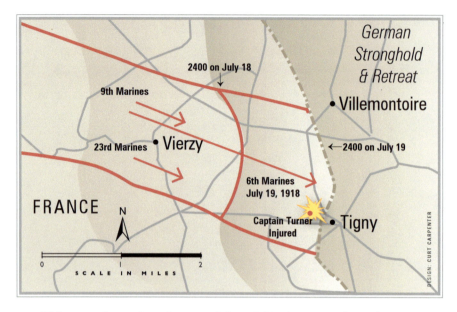

This map shows the advance of the 6th Marines on July 19 that was decidedly brief and bloody. The dot-dash line was as far as they went, and the regiment managed to hang on until a French unit replaced them early the following morning. Captain Turner lost his foot about 300 yards from the small village of Tigny.

REMOVAL AND THE LONG TRIP BACK

IT WAS NOT UNTIL JULY 21—two days later—that Captain Turner arrived at American Red Cross Hospital No. 104 in Beauvais, 68 miles west of Vierzy. He had travelled in a wagon with other badly-wounded men. During that ride, Turner, despite his condition and great pain, continually sat up and talked to the others, bolstering their morale and spirits and wills to live. By the time they reached the hospital, gangrene was setting in his foot and lower leg, requiring the doctors to amputate the leg about six inches below the knee. A later medical report described the wound as a "compound comminuted fracture of the left leg. Amputation of the tibia and fibula at the junction of the middle and lower third was necessary."

Arthur's father in Wilkes-Barre received a telegram from France on July 24, indicating that Captain Turner was in the hospital, but the Marine Command in the States did not know he had been wounded, let alone any particulars. In fact, it was not until a month later, on August 20, that General Barnett at Marine Headquarters telegrammed Arthur's father, telling him, "Deeply regret to inform you cablegram just received states your son Captain Arthur H. Turner Marine Corps severely wounded in action July nineteenth. Impossible at this time to ascertain further particulars...." And, coincidentally, the next day, Arthur's father received a letter from his son that he "had leg shattered below knee and necessitated amputating it." The father requested help getting a passport for Arthur's wife Dorothy "to go over and accompany him home," the request being quickly squelched by the Corps.

Following 18 days in the Beauvais hospital, Arthur was transferred on August 9 to a French 'Mixte' hospital at Alencon, 130 miles to the southwest in Normandy, where he stayed a week, and then on to the U.S. Army hospital at Angers, 85 miles further south, where he remained for 25 days, until September 10. He then began his journey back to the U.S., spending two nights in the U.S. Army Hospital No. 8 in Savenay, and then making the final leg 155 miles to the U.S. Naval Base Hospital No. 5 at Brest, the major port near the tip of Brittany, arriving there on September 13. He moved aboard the U.S.S. *Plattsburg*, which sailed for New York ten days later on September 23.

On September 12, a notice was issued by the Mess Officer of the Savenay Hospital to Arthur, requesting payment for 3 days mess, September 9 to 11, for FF16.95 (equivalent to US$3). This bill caught up to Captain Turner on October 10 in New York, where it was duly paid.

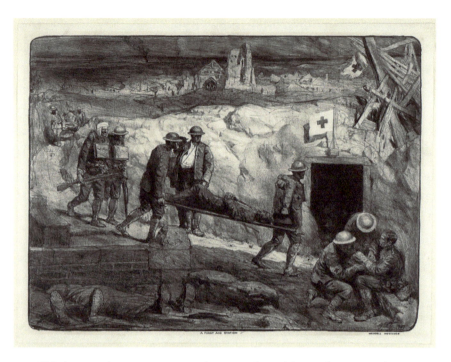

This image shows a cave serving as a first aide station near Vierzy or Beaurepaire Farm for battlefield dressing and triage. This is likely where Captain Turner was initially taken with his shattered foot.

THE SOURCE AND COST OF VICTORY

THERE WERE MANY ACTS OF BRAVERY and heroism, as the Marines had agonizingly but successfully advanced toward Tigny. Several company sergeants led and motivated their men to carry on, despite being seriously wounded. Others—many while wounded—carried wounded comrades to medical help (up to six kilometers away). And still others charged and debilitated enemy machine gun nests that had been mowing down Marines and blocking progress.

A full company consists of 200-250 men, a battalion about 1,000. In a matter of a few hours that morning, more than 70 percent of

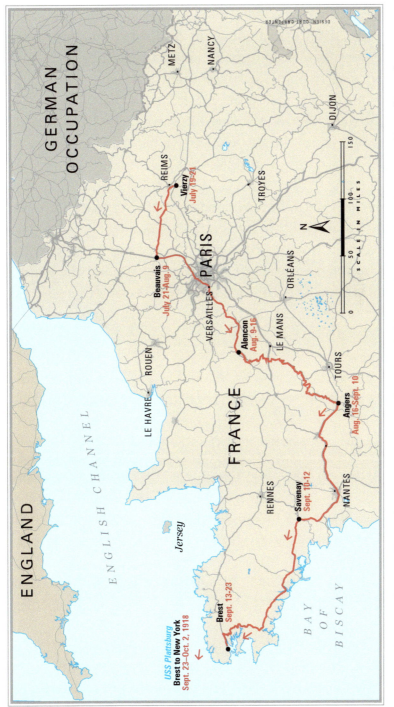

Wounded Captain Turner's 75-day trip home from the field near Vierzy included the cave first aid station and then five different hospitals on French soil before boarding the *Plattsburg*, bound for New York. The amputation evidently took place at Beauvais.

the 1/6 had become casualties—dead, wounded, or missing. Some would return, many would not; many company commanders fell. The losses for the two leading battalions of the 6th Regiment were calculated at more than fifty percent for the day—2,450 Marines marched into battle, 1,150 went out. It is said that Marine casualties here were the worst suffered in a single battle in Marine Corps history—until the battle of the Pacific island of Tarawa in November 1943, during World War II.

As a result of their withered condition, at 3:45 that afternoon, Hughes' 1/6 and the other two battalion commanders were told to advance no further and dig in to hold their ground. Referred to as the "remnants of the 1/6," they were replaced by the French army, and started back through the town. Vierzy was a gas trap, requiring the men to put on their masks—exhausting them even more.

In the single week of July 18-25, 76 officers and 2,015 men became casualties, approximately 43 percent of the entire Marine brigade.

MORE RECOGNITION

FOR HIS ACTION, bravery, and service in the face of the enemy, Captain Turner was awarded the Legion of Honor, the highest honor and award given by the French Government for service to that country.

The award was formalized on December 1, 1918, and reads (translated from the French):

"The Grand Chancellor of the National Order of the Legion of Honor certifies that by decree of December 1, 1918, the President of the French Republic has conferred upon Captain Arthur H. Turner, 6th Regiment Marines the Decoration of Knight in the National Order of the Legion of Honor.

Done in Paris, December 1, 1918
Approved, sealed and recorded No. 20559
The Chief of the Bureau"

The accompanying citation reads, "He gave a noble example of fortitude and stoicism during the engagement which took place near Vierzy on July 19, 1918. Hit by a shell fragment and his leg broken, he insisted in spite of his cruel suffering that the surgeon evacuate the other wounded men first."

Of the 45 Princeton students and alumni serving in the Marines in W W I, Captain Turner was the sole Legion of Honor recipient.

Similarly, Turner's commendation from the A E F 2nd Division reads:

"As Battalion Adjutant, 1st Battalion, 6th Marines, he repeatedly performed services of the most valuable nature during the engagement near Vierzy on the 19th July. In the performance of his duty in the open, struck by a fragment of shell, his leg was shattered. Despite intense pain, he refused to be evacuated for several hours although his life hung in the balance and repeatedly urged the regimental surgeon to evacuate others before him. Knowing that he had lost his leg and full consciousness that he was forever unfitted for active duty for insistence that others should be evacuated before him showed his exalted ideals of a true soldier."

On July 18-19, Captain Turner had "displayed gallantry of the highest order." The French awarded him a second Croix de Guerre with Palm, and the U.S. a second Silver Star for gallantry and a Purple Heart for his injury. Because he had been awarded two Croix de Guerres, for Belleau Wood and Soissons, Turner became eligible to wear the French fourragere on his uniform for the remainder of his Marine Corps career.

On both June 13 and again on July 23, 1918, Colonel Harry Lee, then Commanding Officer of the 6th Marine Regiment, had recommended Captain Turner for the Distinguished Service Cross and other 'suitable reward,' for both his action at Belleau Wood and at Vierzy, which had resulted in the Silver Stars.

Nearly two decades later, in 1937, Colonel John Hughes, Turner's 1st Battalion commander, wrote a letter recommending the Distinguished Service Cross for Turner, but, after further review, the Board of Awards decided the heroism did not justify it, and he had already been recognized by the Silver Star with one oak-leaf cluster.

And, more than twenty five years later, Arthur learned that General James Harbord, who in 1918 commanded the 6th Brigade at Belleau Wood and the entire Second Division at Soissons, had given instructions to have Captain Turner recommended for the Congressional Medal of Honor in July of 1918. Harbord transferred out immediately following the Soissons battle and lost track of the planned recommendation. (He left the service in 1922, and served as President and Chairman of the Radio Corporation of America (RCA) for 25 years until his death in 1947.)

The Legion of Honor certificate, long since waterlogged.

In 1946, Harbord wrote a letter to the Navy Permanent Board of Awards, in support of Arthur being considered yet again for a higher award and for a promotion. In that letter, Harbord notes "the instructions to have him recommended for the Congressional Medal of Honor were either miscarried or imperfectly carried out." He emphasizes Arthur's role and bravery at Soissons, as the point person of the 1/6 on July 17-19. "This officer stayed with his outfit until the Battalion was reduced by casualties to less in numbers than a Company...." And, "He was as far forward in the advance as was reached by anyone in the Division during the battle." Finally, "All of my recollection of those very full days of July, 1918 urges me to lose no opportunity to see justice done to a man who showed the gallantry which

Legion d' honour, Croix de Guerre, Silver Star,
Purple Heart, Marine Expeditionary, 6th Marine Regiment

was exhibited by Major Turner." But, this effort also proved unsuccessful, and additional medals were not forthcoming.

A week after Arthur Turner left the battlefield, Brig. General John Lejeune was appointed to command the Marine Fourth Brigade on July 25, 1918, and declared: "I have this day assumed command of the Fourth Brigade, U.S. Marines. To command this brigade is the highest honor that could come to any man. Its renown is imperishable and the skill, endurance, and valor of the officers and men have immortalized its name and that of the Marine Corps."

Historians have said that the Soissons attack of July 18 and 19 turned the tide. The Germans began a fighting withdrawal east and north from the Marne. Never again in World War One would the German army successfully mount an offensive.

THE HUGHES-TURNER TEAM

CAPTAIN TURNER'S ROLE as the first and only adjutant of the First Battalion, from its inception in July 1917 to his wounding a year later, was important to the 1/6's successes at Belleau Wood and Soissons. Beyond his courage, valor, and effectiveness in the face of the enemy and horrendous mayhem and carnage, he was a constant and steady hand, as the battalion's leadership changed hands eight times in the course of the year: From Major John Hughes to Captain Robert Adams to Major Maurice Shearer to Captain George Stowell and then to Hughes again. And, for some reason, Hughes was also replaced for a single day—June 6 at Belleau Wood—by Major Franklin Garrett, and Garrett stood in for Hughes again from June 14 to July 16, after Hughes was gassed and incapacitated at Belleau Wood.

Turner's effectiveness and heroism was no doubt abetted by having Major (later Colonel) Hughes as his commanding officer for most of the time since the formation of the 1/6 at Quantico. Despite the several absences caused by top-level training courses and temporary debilitation from gas attacks, Hughes was one of the Marine Corps' best and more charismatic leaders. He had joined the Corps in 1900 and prior to 1917, served in the Philippines, Cuba, Panama, and was awarded the Medal of Honor for distinction at Vera Cruz.

He earned his nickname, 'Johnny the Hard' on December 6, 1916, while commanding Marine Barracks in the Dominican Republic. While out hunting for 'insurrectos,' he was shot in the leg, breaking a bone in his shin. Undaunted by the image of his own shin bone jutting out of his leg, he is said to have asked for some wire cutters, cut the protruding bone off, wrapped the leg, and continued the fight. Word got around from his men, and he was 'Johnny the Hard' from then on. The wound had not fully healed when he sailed to France in September 1917. His performance at Belleau Wood and thereafter helped preserve the nickname.

Arthur Turner's small build and thin, high-pitched voice no doubt required him to establish and prove himself in the eyes of his peers and especially down the ranks. As the second-in-command adjutant of the 1/6—on and off horseback—Arthur was perhaps viewed behind his back as a "little fellow" or "little Artie Turner," perhaps all the way back at Quantico. Up until demonstrating his 'out front' courage and heroism at Belleau Wood and Soissons, the demonstrated support of Hughes was important in supporting and reinforcing Captain Turner's authority and auspices as a leader.

It is apparent that the appreciation of military effectiveness, respect, and loyalty was mutual between Major Hughes and Captain Turner.

THE WAR'S END

OVER THE REMAINING FOUR MONTHS of the War— and without Captain Turner—the 1/6 and Fourth Brigade, and the entire Second Division, went on to four major engagements: Marbache Sector (Pont-a-Moussor), August 7-16; St. Mihiel Offensive, September 12-16; Argonne-Meuse (Champagne), October 1-9; and Argonne-Meuse (Argonne Forest), November 1-11. In the Champagne campaign, the Second Division, under General Gouraud, broke the German line at Blanc Mont and ended the four-year pressure on Rheims. Finally, on November 11, 1918, an armistice was signed between the Allies and Germany, bringing the World War to a close.

Following the armistice, the 1/6 marched to and participated in the Allied Occupation of the Rhineland until July 1919, when it was relocated back to Quantico, and then deactivated on August 20, 1919. ✪

PART FOUR

Marine Career and Family Between the Wars

With a wooden leg and new career
as a General Court Martial judge advocate,
Arthur and his new family live in Brooklyn, Haiti,
and Washington, endure the depression years
and, upon his retirement, follow his sons
to their school campuses.

T HE _PLATTSBURG_ docked in New York on October 2, 1918, and Captain Turner was transferred and admitted to the U.S. Naval Hospital at the Brooklyn Navy Yard, and assigned to the Marine Barracks there. Later that month, doctors discovered cellulitis had developed and carried out a small, second operation on the same shin. X Rays showed "a clean operation on bone with no fragments," and Arthur "made an uneventful recovery."

REHABILITATION WITH A NEW LEG

I N MID-NOVEMBER, he was transferred to U.S. Army Hospital No. 3 in Colonia, New Jersey, for reconstruction and rehabilitation. This new hospital was one of the two amputation and artificial limb centers in the eastern U.S. He was fitted with a hardwood prosthetic leg (most likely willow or ash), which he evidently tested right away on a visit to Wilkes-Barre to spend the Thanksgiving holidays with his family near the end of November.

His next medical report, in February, 1919, stated that his "general condition is good. It is believed that further treatment in this case will permit him to take up some form of limited duty." Accordingly, in mid-March, Arthur was transferred back to the Navy Hospital in Brooklyn "for further treatments and disposition" and posted to the Barracks there, where he would work for the next three years.

In June, Arthur arranged a meeting with General Barnett in Washington to discuss a future "light-duty" Marine Corps assignment. He was living in an apartment at 157 Joralemon Street in Brooklyn Heights, about 2 miles from the Yard. Arthur's reasons for requesting light duty in New York City included his need for a second "new leg" and his wish that it be made by the same artisans who made his first one, "they being familiar with my case."

That meeting and Arthur's continued rehabilitation went well. On August 2, General Lejeune appointed Captain Turner to replace the current Judge Advocate of the General Court Martial (GCM) at the Navy Yard. (Lejeune had landed at Vera Cruz the same day as the young Second Lieutenant Turner in April of 1914, and the General also established the Marines American Expeditionary Force at Quantico in 1917. But, it is not certain that the two men ever met.)

BECOMING A JUDGE ADVOCATE

MOST NAVY YARDS had standing general courts martial, of which the presiding officer had no duties other than judicial ones. The court is both judge and jury for the military base, disposing of the law and the facts. At the Brooklyn Navy Yard, Navy Captain K. G. Castleman was president of the GCM, and there were six other members, plus Major Arthur H. Turner acting as judge advocate, or prosecutor. At that time and until the 1960's, judge advocates were line officers with little if any legal background. They served as judges and full members of general and special courts martial, but played the role of leading the prosecution in cases before the courts. And the cases tended to deal exclusively with matters of military justice. Each defendant had the right to select a naval officer as defense counsel or to go outside for a lawyer. "Strict rules of evidence prevail and since the verdict may ruin or salvage a man's whole career, cases frequently are fought as bitterly as any murder trial in outside life." Some cases lasted a month or more.

The General Court Martial was ordered to convene on October 15, 1919, with Captain Turner as judge advocate. The New York Times pointed out that Major Turner "was partially crippled in action in the last war but...has gallantly elected to remain in active service." Although not a lawyer, Captain Turner's capacity to learn and his bent toward organization, precision, and process—combined with his new need for duty that was 'limited' and New York based—proved a good fit with his new assignment. Whether or not he was truly qualified at the beginning, he evidently was good at the job, and turned it into a 25-year career. We do not know his record over those years, in terms of cases decided in favor of, or against, the defendants.

Surprisingly, less than a month later, Lejeune inquired about Arthur's status "with a view to getting him before a Marine Retiring Board." However, his doctors and their medical report from earlier in the year had cleared him for light duty, and it was pointed out that, as a result of a special law governing injuries received in the line of duty, "he cannot be retired if he does not desire it and is able to do other duties than sea duty." Lejeune's office inquired directly to Arthur, who was just starting his GCM duty at the Navy Yard: "Please advise...as to what your wishes are in regard to retirement." Captain Turner responded crisply, "I do not desire to be retired, but wish to remain on the active list of the U.S. Marine Corps.," which Lejeune accepted.

A NEW FAMILY

A YEAR AFTER BEGINNING WORK on the GCM, December 30, 1920 saw the birth of Arthur and Dorothy's identical twin boys, Norman Innes and Donald Charles, the first set of identical twins born at the Nesbitt Memorial Hospital in Kingston, Pennsylvania, just across the Susquehanna River from Wilkes-Barre. Dorothy was living at her parents,' or possibly Arthur's parents' home, in order to deliver the babies locally.

Norman was named after Arthur's British cousin Norman, who had been killed in action in France in 1916 as a member of a Yorkshire regiment. In World War II, son Norman served as a Lieutenant and Lieutenant Commander in the U.S. Navy, being the damage control officer on the battleship U.S.S. *Iowa*. From the *Iowa*, he witnessed the Japanese surrender aboard the adjoining U.S.S. *Missouri* in Tokyo Bay in 1945. And, he served again in the same capacity aboard the U.S.S. *New Jersey* during the Korean War. Norman married Ellen Sue Redinger, and they had four children: Charles Innes, Richard Stephen, Norman

Dorothy Turner and twin boys Norman and Donald in August, 1921.

Paige, and Ellen Jane. After receiving a degree from Rensselaer Polytechnic Institute (RPI), and doing graduate work at the University of Michigan, Norm had a career as an architect at the Southwest Research Institute in San Antonio, Texas, and also maintained a passion for painting, particularly water colors and of boats.

Donald was named in honor of Dorothy's brother, Donald Innes. Donald Turner served as a Lieutenant and Captain in the U.S. Army Air Force, as a navigator ferrying planes across the Atlantic Ocean and around theaters in the Middle East, Africa, and Asia. He married Mary Elizabeth Dow of Hamburg, New York, and they had two children: William Dow and Cynthia Huber. After attending RPI and receiving a degree in psychology from the University of Michigan, Don spent his career in personnel management positions, mostly in Chicago, at a variety of companies in the aircraft, advertising, contact lens, and nuclear power plant design industries.

All military commissions that had been granted as 'temporary' during WWI were revoked as of May 15, 1921, with some individual exceptions. Arthur's promotions to both first lieutenant and captain had been temporary grades, but Arthur was one of those exceptions, no doubt reflecting his desire to make the Marine Corps his career, and his recent duty activation. He was appointed a 'regular commissioned' Captain, as of May 9, 1921.

After two years on the GCM in New York, on March 14, 1922, Captain Turner transferred from the Marine Barracks at the Navy Yard in Brooklyn, to Marine Corps headquarters in Washington, D.C., taking on similar GCM duties there. He evidently requested the transfer, for unknown reasons. Reporting there on April 22 after a brief leave, he, Dorothy and the boys

The handsome couple in Washington in 1923, approximately.
Note the fourragere worn on the Captain's uniform.

lived in the District, not far from his work.

Over the next 2-½ years of GCM duty in Washington, Arthur also served as a Marine Headquarters representative or 'emissary' several times for short periods. In June of 1922, for example, he was sent on the "special, additional assignment" representing Headquarters at the Marine Corps Spring Maneuvers at Gettysburg, Pennsylvania. And in April of 1924, he was sent to the Edgewood Arsenal and Aberdeen Proving Ground in Maryland, "on special temporary duty as observer of gas demonstrations to be held at that place." (Since 1917, the Edgewood area has been used for the development and testing of chemical agent munitions.)

LÉGATION DE LA RÉPUBLIQUE
D'HAITI
WASHINGTON

AU NOM DE LA
RÉPUBLIQUE D'HAITI

PASSEPORT

No. 129

PANAMA RAILROAD CO.
RECEIVED

JUL 29 1924

SECRETARY'S OFFICE

Nous ROBERT LARAQUE Chargé d'Affaires ad interim, délivrons le

présent au Capitaine Arthur M. Turner, U. S. M. C., accompagné de

sa femme et de ses deux enfants, demeurant à Wilkes-Barre, Pa.,

qui l'a réclamé, en déclarant se rendre à Port-au-Prince, Haïti, et

prions les autorités civiles et militaires de leur donner aide et

protection en cas de besoin.

Washington, D. C., le 26 Juillet 1924.

Robert Laraque

The 'visa' for Captain Turner, Dorothy, and the boys from the Haitian
Charge d'Affaires, allowing the family to enter and stay at Port-au-Prince.

POSTING TO HAITI

IN SEPTEMBER OF 1924, Arthur, his wife, and three-year-old twin sons moved to Haiti. He was assigned as 'Brigade Adjutant and Mail Officer' for "garrisoning the Republic of Haiti," to be stationed at Port-au-Prince. They left Pier 65 in New York on the *S.S. Cristobal*. (The *Cristobal* was named for the Panama Canal's Atlantic port city and made the first unofficial trip through the new canal on August 3, 1914. It was one of three sister ships owned by the Panama Railroad Steamship Line, the other two being *S.S. Ancon* and *S.S. Panama*.)

Sons Norm and Don later recalled Arthur venturing onto the front porch in Port-au-Prince each morning with an axe, to 'take care of' large tarantulas that would crawl across the porch and rest to escape the tropical sun.

Arthur's parents visited them in Haiti, enjoying their two grandsons on the beaches and dealing with the maid named 'Intestines.' According to the boys' grandmother, "Don and Norman were always playing soldier when they lived in Haiti." So was Arthur.

A few months after the Turners moved to Port-au-Prince, St. Clements Church in Wilkes-Barre held a special service honoring the 33 residents of its parish who had served in WWI. The service included dedicating a "Te Deum" window and a bronze tablet listing their names. Arthur was included, as was his younger brother Charles Franklin Turner. Called "Pat" (and "Pammie" by close relatives), he had left Princeton in 1916 to be an Army pilot in France. Pammie later became a physician, practicing medicine in Montclair, New Jersey, where he was also the town school system's senior physician for 20 years. His wife's name being Patience, they each called the other 'Pat.'

Although Captain Turner's two-year stint in Haiti was supposed to end in September of 1926, his detachment was reassigned early in May of that year, and Arthur 'negotiated' more than a two-month leave once he returned to the U.S., and before reporting to Washington Marine Headquarters for his next duty.

The family sailed for New York on the *S.S. Panama*, leaving Port au Prince on May 30. (It was intended that he sail on the *Ancon*, but the schedule favored the *Panama*). They arrived in New York on June 4, but Arthur was not to report to Washington Headquarters until July 26, providing more than a seven-week holiday, no doubt some of it spent in the Wilkes-Barre area with all the relations there.

WASHINGTON AND A HEALTH SCARE

ARTHUR DULY REPORTED to Marine Headquarters in Washington, D.C., on July 26, for duty in the Division of Operations and Training. Over the next nearly three years— living in the District at 2035 Rosemont Avenue, N.W.—Arthur was actively involved in General Court Martial activities, and also again was assigned to a variety of special, temporary duties, as well as several Headquarters boards. These boards included "the Examining Board appointed for the purpose of examining applicants for commission in the Marine Corps Reserve," and the Board to examine Warrant Officers. Stints on these boards were located in Washington and his participation ran from the fall of 1926 to June 1929.

Captain Turner's temporary assignments also included regular visits to the Marine Corps school in Quantico, either to participate in instruction, or to monitor and evaluate the courses.

During these years, sons Norman and Donald started school in the District. And each Easter, they took part in the annual Easter egg roll and hunt on the south lawn of the White House. That tradition, begun in 1878, had been cancelled during the War but resumed in 1919.

In 1927, Arthur's bout with a peptic ulcer—and its treatment— was to have important consequences later in his life. The treatment, called Sippy, after the doctor and researcher who invented it, was based on a regimen that included the constant use of whole milk and cream and soft foods, "nightly aspiration of the gastric contents and the hourly administration of alkali." While this treatment evidently greatly relieved Arthur's condition, it was proven through a large clinical test 12 years later to cause a marked increase in myopia. With Arthur's 5/20 vision to begin with (recorded as far back as 1912), any deterioration would present a major problem. And, Arthur steadfastly stuck to the high fat/soft food diet for the rest of his life, far beyond any doctor's advice, with his severe myopia progressing to total blindness in the late 1950's.

RETURN TO BROOKLYN

AT HIS REQUEST, Arthur was transferred from Washington Headquarters to the Brooklyn Navy Yard in the summer of 1929 (reporting on July 15), as judge advocate of the permanent General Court Martial there. The GCM office at the Yard was just inside the Sands Street gate, and shared Building 15 with the Office of the Labor Board.

The family moved into an apartment at 201 East 16th Street in the Flatbush section of Brooklyn, and in the fall of 1929, the eight-year-old boys began attending grade school at P.S. 139, nearby on Rugby Road.

That same fall—in the last week of October—the stock market crash on Wall Street (just across the Brooklyn Bridge from the Navy Yard) marked the beginning of the Great Depression. Unemployment in America rose to 30% by 1933, and the severely weakened economy would last through the 1930s until the build up in anticipation of the Second World War. Undoubtedly thankful to have a secure government service job during the depression, Captain Turner and his still young family continued on with their lives.

Over the next 7 years, Arthur served as a distinguished member and judge advocate of the Navy Yard's GCM. His performance reviews and fitness reports, prepared by several different GCM Presidents, including Navy Captains and Admirals, were regularly 'Outstanding,' with 'particularly desire to have him' marks, and with no adverse or disciplinary mentions.

A letter to Arthur from a retiring President of the Permanent GCM illustrates the effectiveness and relationships that Arthur developed from the early days of his GCM role:

"My dear Major Turner:

I do not like to leave my present duty without a personal expression of the great regret with which I contemplate the severance of our very agreeable nineteen months' association on the General Court Martial.

Under your skillful guidance, the wheels have ground with fineness and with exceeding smoothness and I am deeply appreciative of your never-failing and courteous cooperation and of your able assistance to the Court as its Judge Advocate in helping the President and the Members in their job of dispensing occasional justices. It is the quality and not the quantity of service that counts, and I beg leave to rate the quality of yours very high.

With all best wishes for your happiness and success, I am

Very sincerely yours,
Kenneth G. Castleman,
Captain, U.S. Navy"

With a lifelong affection for French culture, Arthur summarized his abilities with the French language in 1929 as follows:

"- Princeton University 1 year
- MC Institute 80% of course taken to date
- Tutored by French priest in Haiti—1 hour conversation
    twice weekly for about 20 months
- Very slight use one year in France
- Speak and understand only simple expressions very
    slowly spoken; read fluently French classics."

Here, Arthur conveys great modesty—presumably justified—in his French speaking and oral comprehensive ability, while making clear that he could readily comprehend written French. This reflects a successful academic background and keen interest in the language, but also a lack of focus or motivation to learn to converse well.

During all these years and into the 1940's, as his residences moved with his postings and his sons' educational institutions, Arthur gave his alternative residence address—especially while on leave—as his father's 188 West River Street location.

In 1932, Arthur took a U S M C Correspondence 'Special Refresher Course,' in Map Problems, Combat Orders, Map and Aerial Photograph Reading, and Tactics and Technique of Infantry and Associated Arms. His grade average across these courses was 90.42%. Later that year, he completed an Army Extension Course 'Preparatory Subjects and Tactics and Technique of Separate Arms,' for 90 credit hours, scoring 85.90%. Two years later, he took yet another 80-hour Army course, 'Tactical Principles and Decisions,' scoring 80.50%—all this indicating his continuing intellectual interest in the substance of warfare.

In October of 1932—14 years after the close of W W I—Captain Turner was at long last examined for promotion to Major and was found to qualify. However, the upgrade in rank took another year to become effective, with the U.S. military in no hurry in peacetime to promote one-legged officers on light duty. But, the new rank was approved by the new President Franklin Roosevelt, "by and with the advice and consent of the Senate," effective September 1, 1933.

At some point, Chuie began holding Franklin Roosevelt in low esteem, referring to him as "Rosenfelt." There are many possible reasons for this, although all are hypothetical. For example, strongly-conservative Arthur may have opposed F D R's New Deal and other Democratic/liberal policies of his long presidency from 1932 to 1945. Earlier, Roosevelt as governor of New York may have garnered Arthur's political opposition as well. And, before that, FDR had served as Assistant Secretary of the Navy in the Wilson administration during WWI, and perhaps was perceived to be in the anti-war camp. Perhaps Chuie believed FDR's isolationist and neutrality stance and the delay of the U.S. joining WWII until Pearl Harbor was faint-hearted and a mistake. In any case and for whatever reason, Arthur's mispronunciation of Roosevelt's Dutch-derived name was unmistakable and continued through his later life.

The 1934/35 Columbia University Catalog lists Arthur as a student at Columbia's Teachers College, indicating he was continuing to take additional courses.

Sometime in 1935, Arthur suffered from appendicitis and a burst appendix, but recovered quickly and totally.

Sons Donald and Norman moved from P.S. 139 to attend Polly Prep School in Park Slope Brooklyn for eighth or seventh and eighth grades. In the fall of 1935, both fourteen year olds went off to Williston Academy, a private boys preparatory school in Easthampton, Massachusetts. For their first two years there, the boys lived at 212 Main Street, on the edge of the school campus.

During July 1936, the GCM at the Brooklyn Navy Yard moved into more modern offices in Building 14, which they shared with the Marine Corps Brig, a restaurant, and a small garage. Still near the Sands Street Gate, the new location was across Perry Avenue from the Marine Corps Barracks.

In February of 1937, Major Turner was admitted to the Naval Hospital with "discomfort in the amputation stump." He also was found to have 30% loss of hearing in his left ear and 5% loss in his right ear, "of the mixed type as seen on otosclerosis." The report was silent regarding eyesight. The admission report includes the comment, "It is believed this Officer will not return to active duty," and declares him "Unfit for service" without explanation, concluding with the "Recommendation that he be ordered to appear before a Naval Retiring Board." However, the report also indicates that "This patient desires retirement from active duty." So it could be that the examining doctors were sympathetic and gave him the recommendation he wanted. He had passed the 20-years-of-service milestone, which provided an increase in his potential military pension.

He left the hospital for four days at the end of March to appear before the Naval Retiring Board in Washington. The Board 'granted' his retirement, and he was returned to hospital with orders to continue treatment and then proceed home. He was discharged from hospital on May 4, and formally placed on the Marine officers' retired list, "relieved from all active duty in the Marine Corps," on July 1, 1937. He was just shy of 50 years old.

RETIREMENT AND NEW TOWNS

ARTHUR SPECIFIED his home address as 201 East 16th Street in Brooklyn until July 1, 1937, and, thereafter, 239 Main Street, Easthampton, Massachusetts. Immediately upon retiring, Arthur and Dorothy left 16th Street, and Brooklyn after eight years, and moved to the Main Street address in East-hampton—just down the street from Williston—to be with the boys and reduce their living costs.

But, before leaving Brooklyn that summer, Arthur bought a new black or gray 4-door Packard at Berry Motor Co. on Flatbush

The type of new, 1937 Packard Arthur bought upon retiring from the Marine Corps, and that he would drive for at least the next 15 years.

Avenue. (As his wooden leg was the left one, Arthur was able to navigate both the clutch and accelerator with his right foot.)

The boys graduated from Williston in June 1939, and, that fall, matriculated as engineering students at Rensselaer Polytechnic Institute (RPI), in Troy, New York, near Albany and only 80 miles from Easthampton.

The next spring, in May of 1940, the Marine Corps Major General Commandant offered Arthur an active duty assignment as Officer in Charge of the Recruiting District of Springfield, Massachusetts, "to report no later than 6 June, 1940." Assignment of retired officers to active duty was under a then existing "limited national emergency," presumably reflecting the war building up in Europe. There is no indication that he took or even seriously considered the assignment.

Arthur's disinterest in the Recruiting District job may well have reflected his and Dorothy's desire to remain close to and involved with their sons' home life and schooling. For, three months later, in August of 1940, Arthur and Dorothy moved from Easthampton to 1697 Tibbits Avenue, Troy, New York, where Donald and Norman were about to be sophomores at RPI.

Arthur had a tonsillectomy sometime in 1940, at age 52.

Donald left RPI after two years, in order to prepare to enter the military and World War II, but Norman remained at RPI and received his Bachelor's degree in Architecture in 1942. Both entered officer candidate programs, after working on a farm in Sullivan County New York and gorging on carbohydrates for a few months, in order to gain weight necessary to qualify for the service. Donald became a Second Lieutenant and navigator in the Army Air Corps, and Norman an Ensign in the Navy.

In March 1942, Arthur's mother, Delphine—nicknamed Mimmi— died at her West River Street home in Wilkes-Barre, at age 73. ✪

239 Main Street, Easthampton, Massachusetts, on the edge of the Williston Academy campus, where Arthur and Dorothy took up residence after his 1937 retirement.

1697 Tibbits Avenue in Troy, New York, where Arthur and Dorothy were to live for two years, while the boys atended RPI and then left for the war.

PART FIVE

Duty Again, in Brooklyn

*Major Turner rejoins the Corps
to assist the World War Two effort
as a member of the General Court Martial
at the burgeoning Brooklyn Navy Yard,
living in a rented house nearby.*

I N AUGUST OF 1942, eight months after the attack on Pearl Harbor and the U.S. entry into World War II, the Navy asked Arthur to return to active duty as a member of the GCM at the Brooklyn Navy Yard. With the boys departed from RPI and Troy, and the U.S. war effort well under way, Arthur readily agreed. He passed his physical exam at the Springfield, Massachusetts station (with height of 5' 8", weight at 118 pounds, and 5/20 uncorrected vision). On October 14, at age 55, Major Arthur H. Turner was back in the Marine Corps for the third time, rejoining the other seven members of the standing General Court Martial at the Navy Yard.

With the war on, the Yard was building military vessels from scratch and repairing others all during the War, with peak

The court in September 1944, in its office in Building 14 at the Navy Yard. Major Turner is at far right. Several fellow court members had been peers of Major Turner in World War I, but were now of higher rank, partly because Turner's ineligibility for combat duty due to his leg wound limited him to a single promotion.

employment around the clock. And, the G C M was busy during those years.

With Arthur working in Brooklyn again, and he and Dorothy now 'empty nesters,' they moved back to Brooklyn. They rented a three-bedroom apartment comprising the first and half the third floors of a three-story house built in 1910, at 550 Argyle Road, near Newkirk Plaza in the Flatbush section of Brooklyn. They were to reside there for the next three decades. Their five-year-old Packard was in the small, detached garage next to the house.

Life at the Yard was exciting and, of course, offered Arthur direct participation in the war effort, despite being far from the theaters of engagement. The Yard was a city in itself, wholly focused on winning the war. 70,000 workers, distributed in round-the-

550 Argyle Road in Brooklyn, where Arthur and Dorothy
occupied the ground floor and the rear half of the third
floor from October 1942, until the summer of 1970.

clock shifts, came and went daily, entering through the main
gates with their identification cards and parcels checked by
Marine guards. Through most of the war, ships were docked
several deep at the piers. New ship construction, augmented by
loadings and un-loadings, repair crews of welders and steel cutters, the many cranes and trucks, and the ever-present trains
traversing the extensive internal rail system all made the Yard
a frenetic and noisy place. Smells from all of these operations,
combined with the sea and river air, added to the industrious
and can-do atmosphere.

The Yard also serviced wounded warships from other Allied
countries. And, atop and adjoining the taller buildings were
towers and antennas that were central to the Navy's Atlantic
Fleet radio communications network.

Although some women had worked in the Yard as secretaries and nurses over the years, the decision was made in the summer of 1941 to help meet the need for skilled labor by hiring women for true 'production' jobs, including mechanics, technicians, welders, machinists, and many others. (Thus, the national 'Rosie the Riveter' campaign during those years, although the poster girl was from the Philadelphia Navy Yard.)

One of the best views of it all was from the top of Building 77, then a relatively new city block size storage structure without windows except for the top four of its 16 floors. Facing north, across the site's 300 acres and towards the East River and Manhattan, one could see the entire Yard panorama, from the Commandant's house and shipbuilding ways to the west, to past Pier K and the barge basin to the east, and all the buildings, roadways, cranes, dry docks and piers in between. As author Jennifer Egan portrays, anyone gazing from those windows during those years, observing all that military might and industrial activity, could not help but ask: "How can we not win?"

Beyond the Yard in Brooklyn, the rest of New York City was consumed by the war as well. Sailors, Army soldiers, officers of all the services, and foreign service men were all over Manhattan and the other boroughs. Although newspapers were banned from the Yard, "for fear of damaging morale," daily news barkers, newspaper kiosks, and the moving messages in Times Square kept track of progress and setbacks around the world.

Prominent among the activities and accomplishments at the Yard during those years were the launchings of two Iowa-class battleships and five aircraft carriers, all built there between August 1942 and October 1945. The launchings were major

LAUNCHING
BATTLESHIP
U.S.S.MISSOURI

NAVY YARD, NEW-YORK
JAN. 29,1944.

The program for launching the U.S.S. *Missouri* at the Brooklyn
Navy Yard on January 29, 1944, an event that the Turner's
no doubt attended. Senator Harry S. Truman spoke, and his
young daughter Margaret christened the ship. 19 months later,
Japan would surrender to the Allies aboard the *Missouri*.

events and celebrations, and the Major and Dorothy likely attended most of them.

Arthur's cases as GCM judge advocate were of course driven by accusations of military malfeasance, a necessary but somewhat depressing or downbeat facet of Navy life and operations. However, the role, contribution, energy, and excitement of the Yard during the Major's WWII years there must have offset feelings of marginality or distance from the overseas battlefields.

Sixty-five years later, the Brooklyn Navy Yard continues to expand as a successful industrial park in New York City, with its five piers, six dry docks, and centuries-old naval legacy still very much in tact. The Yard was deactivated and sold to the City in 1966. The long-closed Naval Hospital, where Major Turner

The Naval Hospital on its own 25-acre campus at a corner of the Brooklyn Navy Yard, where Captain Turner recovered from his battle wounds and spent upwards of 30 weeks for various infirmities over his 30-year Marine Corps career. Closed by the 1970s, the building will soon be a prominent piece of the Yard's new 'media campus.'

recovered after World War I and thereafter visited sporadically while living in Brooklyn, is a landmarked building that will soon be renovated and leased as an integral part of a media, technology, and film production campus at the Yard. Building 14, which housed the General Court Martial offices was raised many years ago. Although the current Yard is booming with 300 resident businesses and will grow its employment from 12,000 now to 20,000 over the next few years, it is difficult to imagine 70,000 daily workers coming and going in the years Major Turner was there during W W I I.

In February of 1944, Arthur's father died at Nesbitt Memorial Hospital in Pennsylvania, at age 86. He was a long-time member and supporter of the St. Stephens Episcopal Church in Wilkes-Barre, and also a long-time Shriner, or Mason, at the Irem Temple fraternal organization in Wilkes-Barre. Arthur also participated at Irem over the years, with his ornate, impressively constructed and Brooklyn-made fez.

At the beginning of 1945, Major Turner took up temporary duty as judge advocate of a special G C M at U.S. Naval District Headquarters at 90 Church Street in Manhattan, in addition to

Arthur's Irem Temple fez, finely made in Brooklyn.

his regular duties at the Yard G C M. Most of that January was dedicated to two important trials convened at the Third District Headquarters, of Captain Charles D. Edmunds and Lieutenant Walter M. Metcalf, both Navy officers.

On August 22, 1945, seven days after Japan's agreement to surrender and end World War II—but still 10 days prior to the formal surrender—the Marine Corps notified Arthur that he would be returned to inactive status, detached from his G C M station and duties, directed to proceed home on September 14, and resume his status on the retired list as of November 11.

However, Arthur and the G C M had just begun a case involving Lieutenant Commander Equen B. Meader, requiring the extension of his active service.

> "The case is an involved, lengthy, and important one. There are twelve charges embracing one hundred and one specifications. ... The prosecution does not expect to close its case much before the end of the month. No estimate of the time the defense expects to take is available, although it is hoped that the case may be finished by the middle of September."

Meader was charged with stealing 180 weapons while on post in Algiers in North Africa and sending them to his home in Forest Hills, New York. He cited a hobby of collecting firearms; the Government countered, "he also made a hobby of collecting government property." The Navy said this was "the largest theft ever charged to an individual in a court martial."

The case lasted longer, and as a result, Major Turner was finally 'detached' four months later on January 4, 1946, granted 69 days of final leave, and "Resumed status on retired list and issued Certificate of Satisfactory Service" on March 15, 1946.

In Arthur's six Fitness Reports between rejoining the New York GCM in 1942 and his 1946 retirement, GCM President Rear Admiral Lamar Leahy gave him more "outstanding" and "particularly desire to have him" ratings. Leahy's comments include: "An outstanding officer—able and reliable;" and "An excellent officer in every way. It has been a special pleasure to have him serve with me;" and "Major Turner is an outstanding officer particularly well fitted for this type of duty."

The Admiral stated on a 1945 Report: "Outstanding and thoroughly qualified for promotion." Records indicate that over the three years 1943 to 1945, Major Turner was considered for promotion to Lt. Colonel nine times, and was 'Passed Over' each time. It is unclear whether Arthur knew he was being considered. ✪

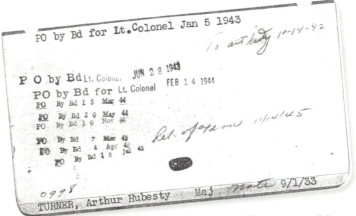

The note card from
AHT's military file indicating 9 dates of consideration for promotion to Lieutenant Colonel between January 1943 and June 1945, and 9 'Passed Over' (PO) notations.

PART SIX

Real Retirement and Sightlessness

Adopting a quiet retirement at the War's end,
Arthur and Dorothy remain in Brooklyn for 25 years,
during which Arthur loses his sight, and spend their last years
in hometown Wilkes-Barre and then near their son in Texas.

OLD ISSUES OF MEDALS AND RANK

I MMEDIATELY AFTER RETIRING, Arthur tried to prompt action on a possibly botched Medal of Honor award, as well as on a possible promotion as a retiree. The issues were triggered, or at least fueled, by Lt. General J. G. Harbord—who commanded the Second Division during Soissons—telling Turner and writing to the Navy Board of Awards in 1946, that he had recommended Turner for the Congressional Medal of Honor in 1918, and suggesting that they consider it once again.

Arthur believed and made a case that an English citation meant for the Medal of Honor was improperly used as a translation of the French Legion of Honor award and not forwarded with his Medal of Honor recommendation. This hypothesis was somewhat supported by confusion and miscommunication back in 1918 in the gallantry and citation recommendations between

AEF commands and Marine Headquarters. And, in 1922, the War Department had to correct the original English language citation for the French Legion of Honor, to the proper translation from the French.

As has already been described, after further review in 1946, the Board of Decorations and Medals did find a 1918 recommendation for at least one Distinguished Service Cross for Turner's service, but they found no Medal of Honor recommendation. And, they denied any further awards.

Regarding the issue of being promoted only once since 1918—and that on the basis of seniority before retirement—the Acting Secretary of the Navy declared Arthur was ineligible for promotion "by reason of having been specially commended for performance of duty in actual combat." In essence, his long history of 'light duty,' no matter how successful, did not count toward promotion.

MAINTAINING A BROOKLYN HOME

ARTHUR AND DOROTHY continued to live at their Flatbush apartment. They had depended on Arthur's Marine Corps earnings throughout his career, and now his pension for retirement. In retirement, this allowed them to live quietly comfortably, especially at first. His monthly pension was $315, which was about 50% higher than the average U.S. income at the time, with new cars selling for $1,125, and the average house for $5,150.

Arthur never filed or paid income taxes and did not acquire a Social Security number until 1970, evidently remaining completely off the tax rolls. The family discovered this only when son Norman needed to establish a Social Security number, in order to apply for Medicare benefits on behalf of Arthur after he moved to San Antonio. Arthur's retirement pay was exempt from income tax, and he never had material other income that was taxable.

They always rented and never owned a home, and the momentum of living at Argyle Road in Brooklyn during and after World War II kept them there for 30 years. Arthur looked into taking advantage of W W I I Veterans Administration (VA) home mortgage loans. But, he did not follow through—perhaps content with his Brooklyn arrangement, and perhaps for lack of a down payment or income sufficient to carry a loan.

With the limited pension income, they lived increasingly modestly and frugally. They ate out rarely and travelled relatively little. Over the decades, Arthur and Dorothy spent summer vacations with his sister Edith at her comfortable 'tiny cottage' house in the woods on Pioneer Avenue about 8 miles north of Wilkes-Barre in Shavertown, Pennsylvania. Although the two sons and their families did not live permanently in the area, several cousins and their broods remained there in the Wyoming Valley through at least the 1960s. And, Dorothy's sister, Marion Ross, also lived nearby, on Wyoming Avenue in Kingston.

And, in the early 1950s, Arthur and Dorothy made summer visits to their son Norman's home just outside Boston. In 1955, they visited Norm and Sue in San Antonio, Texas, as they were considering moving down there so Norm could become the chief architect at the new and promising Southwest Research Institute. Arthur and Dorothy used every argument to try to convince them not to leave New England for life at the "last outpost of civilization"—Texas. This may have helped convince

Norm and Sue to move; in any case, they did move and spent the rest of their lives in San Antonio, delighted.

Edith may well have provided financial support over the years, and she gave Arthur her used 1949 Chrysler in 1953 or 1954, to replace his 16-year-old Packard. Despite poor and declining eyesight, Arthur drove the Chrysler for a number of years between Brooklyn and Wilkes-Barre, Boston, and cities farther afield. He kept the car until the fall of 1964, a half dozen years after he lost his sight.

In 1968, Edith also gave Arthur a significant—but unknown—amount of money to ease his financial situation. In response, he wrote:

> "Your very nice, interesting letter containing your very very generous magnificent check has just arrived and I cannot thank you enough, dear sister, for your kindness and thoughtfulness in sending this to me. It will place us in a much more comfortable position than we have been for some time."

One of the reasons for the immediacy of Arthur's reply to his sister was to return her check, which she had forgotten to sign!

During the 1950s and 1960s, the grown sons and their families paid sporadic visits to the Brooklyn house. In the early 1950s, Chuie took a grandson via subway to a Brooklyn Dodgers baseball game at Ebbets Field. And, on another occasion, he took son Don and his young son to the Navy Yard and aboard the Essex class aircraft carrier U.S.S. *Wasp*, which was in for repairs.

Arthur and his family, c. 1924
Front Row: **Margaret Townend, Donald Turner,** *(Arthur's son)*
Norman Turner *(son),* **James Turner;**
Second Row: **Charles Simpson Turner** *(father),* **Ernest Townend, Jr.,**
Dorothy Turner *(wife),* **Delphine Turner** *(mother),* **Patience Turner;**
Back Row: **Arthur Hubesty Turner, Charles Franklin Turner** *(brother),*
Edith Turner Townend *(sister)*

Also, a few times during that period, when the sons were in town, Arthur and Don would play their violins, with Norman at the piano. The history of their learning the instruments has been lost, but all three apparently took their lessons early in life and greatly appreciated classical music—not only to play, but also as a listening pastime. (Don and Norm also liked to dance to the big bands of the 1930s and 1940s, as Sammy Kaye and other bands toured from city to city.)

BLINDNESS

IN ADDITION to living with an artificial leg since 1918, Arthur lost his sight completely by 1958, almost certainly from a vitamin or other deficiency acquired through the prescribed high-cholesterol 'special diet' of the Sippy Treatment he adopted for his peptic ulcer in 1927—but then failed to discontinue, years after the diet was no longer appropriate. He continued to eat primarily eggs, butter by the slice, pureed and baby food, and the like, for the rest of his life.

Sightless, Chuie navigated his apartment with ease, having memorized every piece of furniture and every conceivable path around his six-room home. He had a morning regimen for years that included a set of in-place exercises, stretching, massaging his gums, and affixing his wooden leg. Grandsons recall helping him strap on the leg each morning, going for walks around his Flatbush neighborhood, and shopping with him, including for a new, red rubber tip for his cane.

Despite acute myopia dating back to his early years and progressing to total blindness, there are no indications that he ever wore corrective lenses of any kind. That is, no military and family pictures, personal recollections, prescriptions, or descriptions show or describe any glasses belonging to or used by Chuie. Although two Marine Corps medical exam reports refer to his "corrected" and "corrected by glasses" vision, even those reports do not mention or provide any evidence of lenses being prescribed or used, beyond the examining room.

FINAL MOVES

IN 1970, Dorothy was 86 years old and Arthur 82, blind, and with a wooden leg. Yet, they still lived alone, and Dorothy did

A central residential area of Wilkes-Barre during the 1972 flood.

their limited cooking, in a residential but still busy New York City neighborhood.

But, in the summer of that year, after nearly 30 years at 550 Argyle Road, they moved back to Wilkes-Barre, renting a new, two-bedroom ground-floor apartment at 143 Barney Street, about a mile and a half from both the Public Square and the river. Arthur quickly mastered the new place and was just as mobile and quasi self-reliant there, despite never having set eyes on the property.

Just two years on, in June 1972, tropical storm Agnes pushed the Susquehanna River—which runs through the middle of town— to a height of nearly 41 feet, four feet above the city's levees. The entire downtown was flooded with nine feet of water, with the level reaching the ceiling of the Turner apartment, despite the building being more than a mile from the riverbank. A total of

Arthur and Dorothy's house at 143 Barney Street, where
the flood waters reached the second floor and ren-
dered most first floor apartments uninhabitable.

128 deaths were attributed to the storm, the majority from the
drowning of persons trapped in their cars.

When rescuers came around to help evacuate the Turners from
their rapidly flooding home, Arthur thought they were exagger-
ating the danger and did not want to go. So, the sheriff hoisted
him over his shoulder and removed the couple by motorboat,
delivering them to a temporary shelter in a school building on
dry land across the river.

Following the flood and the loss of their apartment, Arthur and
Dorothy moved to Oak Hills Haven, an assisted living residence
in San Antonio, near son Norman and his family. Although he
had developed skin and perhaps other cancers over a period
of years, Arthur died of a cerebral vascular hemorrhage in San

Three-man Marine Corps color guard, after formally present-
ing Dorothy with an American flag in honor of Chuie's service.

Antonio, on September 9, 1972, at age 84, only three months
after moving there.

At his interment service at the Prince of Peace Episcopal Church
in Dallas, Pennsylvania, Dorothy was presented with a folded,
U.S. Capitol-flown American flag by a Marine Corps color guard
in a typically formal, impressive, and emotional 30-second pre-
sentation in honor of his service to his country.

Dorothy, suffering from Alzheimer's disease, lived in a nursing
home facility in San Antonio, until passing away from cardiac
arrest on February 28, 1976. She was 92. Arthur and Dorothy
are buried next to his parents in the Grand View Lawn section
of the Evergreen Cemetery in Shavertown, Pennsylvania, about
eight miles from Wilkes-Barre. ✪

ARTHUR HUBESTY
TURNER
OCT. 13, 1887
SEPT. 9, 1972

DOROTHY INNES
TURNER
MAY 7, 1883
FEB. 28, 1976

EPILOGUE

We all play a part in history,
and the confluence of world forces and events,
and Arthur Turner's early development and life decisions,
made his place in history special.

A PLACE IN HISTORY

THE WAR

WORLD WAR I changed the course of history in many ways, being the bloodiest and most brutal war to date; representing the transition from largely hand-to-hand combat aided by cannons, to the increasingly high-tech conflict of future wars; propelling the emergence of the United States as a dominant world power; and sowing the seeds for a second world war one short generation later. So, W W I—and those who participated in it—mattered.

THE BATTLES

IN THE COURSE of that war, certain battles appear to have been particularly pivotal, in affecting and effecting the outcome. Historians cite the Battle of Belleau Wood and the Soissons attack as turning points of the war in Europe, from four years of defense and trench-bound standoffs and slaughter, to an Allied offensive wave that quickly moved eastward to the armistice and war's end, only 16 weeks later. So, the events of June and July 1918 mattered a lot.

THE MARINE CORPS

I N PLAYING the central and lead roles at Belleau Wood and Soissons, the U.S. Marine Corps established itself as an equal—they would claim the premier—service within the American military. This was a dramatic improvement and expansion from what had become a moribund and somewhat vestigial force from the days of naval sailing ships.

The accomplishments at the 1918 battles, and the respect and awe for the officers and men who fought in them, have benefitted the Marine Corps to the present day, with the Corps' reputation for resolve and effectiveness reinforced in mythic terms. So, the Marine Corps mattered in W W I, and W W I mattered to the standing and future of the Marine Corps.

THE MAJOR

W E DO NOT KNOW exactly why or how Arthur Turner developed such a passion to stop the Axis powers and participate in the War so early on, nor do we know why he sought to be a Marine Corps officer with similar passion. But, those passions and objectives were real, and he pursued and achieved them both, starting five years before his country entered W W I.

As a result, and with the serendipitous and coincidental timing of his readiness and the unfolding of the Western Front events in mid-1918, he was thrust into those horrific but critical battles, and he rose to the challenge.

Although the importance of his role and contributions may be burnished to some degree by the fact that he survived the battles, his gallantry and full participation in the successes cannot be denied or diminished. The praise of his unit, the quoted and official praise from his superior officers, and the medals and citations awarded to him by the American and French governments speak for themselves. So, Chuie mattered.

In summary, Arthur Turner played an important role in the Marine Corps, which led two critical battle victories in 1918, which led to the Allied victory in W W I, which, in turn, changed the world.

HEALTH

ARTHUR'S LIFE HISTORY risks painting him as small, sickly, and feeble, but that was not the case. He was indeed slight in stature, and he acquired and suffered many maladies, including an early hearing deficiency, significant and progressive myopia by age 25, a lasting peptic ulcer at age 39, a burst appendix at age 47, a tonsillectomy at age 52, a hernia at 59, total blindness in his 70s, and cancer in his 80s.

But, he lived 84 years, and successfully fought through and overcame most of those afflictions. Strength, stamina, and other essential physical requirements were never an issue joining the Marine Corps or serving on the battlefields—he must have been a bit of a bulldog and not too big a target. The blindness, of course, was an exceptional limitation, and having the world turned to darkness curtailed much of his daily activities, including driving, reading, and going out and about independently. But, this did not occur until he was in his 70s, and he remained able to drive and be mobile until then. And, inside his homes, he got around very well on his own, albeit, of course, with constant attention and care from Dorothy.

There is no evidence, anecdotes, family stories or even rumors indicating that he may have suffered from posttraumatic stress disorder (PTSD) from his experiences in the trenches and on the battlefields. Many others did suffer from what was previously referred to as shell shock and battle fatigue, and it is difficult to believe that memories of his worst experiences in France were not relived in some form. But even among his family and close friends, there evidently was no outward sign that the trauma took its toll psychologically after WWI.

He rarely brought up war subjects himself, preferring to respond to questions that might be put to him. But he was amenable— and often eager—to describe his wartime activities, and could do so in poignant and minute detail.

CAREER AND LIFESTYLE

WE ARE NOT SURE and have little evidence about what kind of career Arthur wanted or aspired to. He attended excellent schools, earned his engineering degree, and then seemingly embarked on a promising career as a civil engineer. But his first jobs were brief—barely three years—and he never went back to that work. We do not know whether his joining the Marines in 1912 reflected a desire for a career in the military, or only the best way to help win the brewing war, without a potentially long-term commitment in mind. Thereafter, we are not sure what he had in mind or considered as a career beyond WWI, or beyond the Marine Corps, if anything, and if ever. There certainly is no evidence that he joined the Marines "for the purpose of aiding his personal ambitions," as has been ascribed to many military officers of that era.

It is clear that he was well suited for, and became successful— and happy, one must assume—with his General Court Martial work, which he began as he was still recovering from his wounds, and sustained for more than 25 years. He may have asked to be appointed to the Navy Yard G C M, or General Lejeune may have had the idea as a good way to meet both the Corps and Arthur's needs.

In any case, the job allowed him to remain in the Marine Corps and mostly in New York. The nature of the work—project based, with legalistic procedures and analytical rigor—appears to have matched Arthur's interests. He was good at it, and no doubt was a fair but tough, disciplined, and disciplining G C M judge advo- cate. (One family member recalls "feeling sorry for the service- men who had to stand before him as a judge in military court in Brooklyn.") He knew he was adding value. And, so did his supe- riors, who included officers at the top of the Marine Corps and Navy ranks. The job also enabled him to contribute to W W I I, five years after his first retirement.

Although the two world wars and Arthur's participation in them were very different affairs, they in a sense represent 'bookends' of his active and rewarding 30-year Marine Corps career. His role in W W I was squarely in harms way at the Front, overseas and in the face of the enemy and its bayonets, gas, and cannon. Whereas in W W I I, he was thousands of miles from any front and worked in an office five miles from home. In W W I, he was a leader of men, lost a leg, and was decorated for bravery, gallantry, and victory. Whereas in W W I I, his personal contribution was to the Navy and Marine Corps legal system, and much more indirectly to the war effort itself (although the vicarious contribution of having two sons serving as officers in the Middle East and Asia was not lost on him). He no doubt felt honored, lucky, and enthusiastic to be called back in 1942 to play a legitimate and expert role, and was rewarded with a U.S. victory in the war and two returning, healthy sons.

To our knowledge, he never wanted to pursue anything else. He may have quickly become disillusioned with civil engineering, and never seriously considered business in general or his father's importing and manufacturing company as potential careers. Once in the Marine Corps, and having attained a pinnacle on the battlefield at age 30, the momentum of his initial judge advocate assignment probably helped turn GCM into a career. But to him, the Marine Corps was the career.

Money or a high life style did not appear to be a goal, and Arthur did not outwardly display resentment or envy of others who had more means or were 'living bigger.' Some family members and good friends (mostly in and around Wilkes-Barre) were successful and wealthy doctors, lawyers, and businessmen, while Arthur was a Major in the Marines. All seemed to respect one another.

Arthur and Dorothy made do and limited their lifestyle and activities to what they could afford. They never owned a house, were frugal with clothes and all other possessions, and took few vacations and few trips anywhere other than to their Pennsylvania home town and to visit a few other relatives. Christmas and birthday gifts were heart felt and well-remembered, and sometimes for the grandchildren included a few dollars, maybe a pack of chocolate cigars from Barricini, and once in a while a set of British-made miniature lead soldiers.

Arthur and Dorothy were seemingly happy and content with their lifestyle and financial lot. However, at least a few times, his sister Edith and perhaps others in the family generously helped them out to keep them away from suffering or destitution.

FAMILY

ARTHUR MAINTAINED close relationships with his brother and sister throughout his life, especially Edith, who resided in Wilkes-Barre her whole life and was his closest friend and relative. (She was also the 'matriarch' of the extended Turner family until she died in 1974 at age 88.) She always kept in touch with her 'dearest Chuie' and Dorothy, as well as helping out in many ways throughout his life, not the least of which was hosting the couple regularly at her home. In the mid-1950s, Edith gave Chuie her Chrysler, and then there was the significant check in 1968, shortly after Chuie turned 80.

Wilkes-Barre remained the family home front that Arthur and Dorothy often visited over the decades—no matter where he was stationed or where they actually resided.

Arthur and his brother and sister were the first of his line born in America. They were children of an English immigrant father who settled in a middle-sized coal mining town during the industrial revolution, married a local lady from a farming family, developed a successful business, and sent his children to private schools and then off to college. Sister Edith married a prominent local businessman, Arthur's brother Pat became a doctor in New Jersey, and Arthur was a career military officer elsewhere.

Although his heart always remained with his family and Wilkes-Barre, Arthur really never again resided there after leaving for Princeton in 1904, until he moved back for two years at age 82. And his two sons attended schools and colleges in New York City, Massachusetts, New York State, and Michigan, and never lived in Pennsylvania (although they, too, visited often when they were boys and young adults). The sons and their subsequent families 'went west,' to Illinois and Texas.

So, in a sense, Arthur and his brother, as first generation Americans, dispersed the family from its Wilkes-Barre origins.

ATTITUDE AND DISPOSITION

ARTHUR TURNER embodied perhaps a rare combination of characteristics, on the one hand being firm, tough, stoic, stern, severe, and bull-headed; but, on the other, being engaging, interested, caring, and 'a sweetheart.'

In many respects, his life seems to have been bifurcated into two eras with the transition from one to the other marked by the Minenwerfer HE shell explosion that shattered his leg on July 19, 1918. Prior to that—in his first 30 years—Arthur grew up and took advantage of a relatively privileged life in a successful merchant family. He was alert, active, driven, good at studies, keen to go away to college to study engineering, and active in college (fencing, baseball manager, studying French). He changed colleges, moved to the 'big city' of Boston, graduated, took initial jobs farther afield (Atlanta), traveled to the United Kingdom and France, aggressively pursued and joined the Marine Corps (twice) as an officer, served in Latin America, married Dorothy, and pursued the war effort in Europe. That was the first era.

In the second era, for the next 54 years following the Soissons battle, he was confined physically, had a desk job, found and flourished in his GCM role and moved from one GCM to another (in New York, Haiti, Washington, New York), lived in the boys' school locations (Easthampton and Troy), stayed at 550 Argyle for 28 years, maintained few friends beyond the family, lost his sight and stopped driving, and was limited in what he could do by modest financial resources.

Much of this shift can be attributed to the loss of his leg—and blindness much later—and the natural aging process contributed as well. During the second era, Arthur was a competent, respected, and successful judge advocate. He took military courses that were not required, and rejoined the Marine Corps in 1942 for WWII. His strong relationships with Dorothy and his other relatives never waned, and he spent occasional time with grandchildren.

Arthur made the shift better than most. He seems to have been happy with his lot, maintained a good sense of humor, displayed contentment, and maintained genuine family relationships and loyalty throughout those last 54 years.

This is not to say he was easy to get along with, and some family members tolerated, rather than enjoyed his company. Virtually all his relatives loved him and greatly respected his valor, contributions, and sacrifice for the country in WWI, but more than one was not pleased to be with him. When he was staying at his sister's 'tiny cottage,' others dreaded going there, as there was only one bathroom and Chuie "spent nearly all morning in it. Others would have to go in the bushes." And, despite being a picky eater who needed everything pureed for him, he would be quick and severe to criticize his sister—his generous and tolerant hostess—for serving dishes he disliked to others. He was often arrogant and outspokenly hyper-critical and rarely changed his often strong opinions.

Although these behaviors could be attributed to an underlying anger or PTSD from WWI, they are similar to the essence of his dressings down by the Marine Corps during his officer training program way back in the summer of 1914. In any case, the sternness and rigidity seemed to mellow in his later years and he became more docile after going blind.

Although the issues of being passed over for the Medal of Honor, Distinguished Service Cross, and an additional promotion, appear to have gnawed at Arthur in his later life, the Legion of Honor award by the French government imbued in him a lasting pride and sense of honor, and at least partially offset the perceived slight by his own country. His long-standing affinity for French history and culture, and that country's appreciation of his service in June and July 1918, made that award a pinnacle of patriotism and recognition for Arthur, no matter what the American military and government did or did not do. For the rest of his life, whenever he wore civilian clothes, his suit coats and sport jackets were adorned with the small, deep red lapel buttonhole ribbon, as was the custom for Legion of Honor recipients in and outside France.

Many old people are accused, often justifiably, of living in the past. In Arthur Turner's case, in many ways—and probably in his own mind—his life's greatest or most consequential 'work' and event comprised the 1918 battles. Relative to those victorious battles, his GCM work, life with his family, and retirement

Major Turner, with sons Navy Lt. Commander Norman and
Air Force Captain Donald, in Brooklyn in February 1946, following
World War II and one month before the Major's final discharge

.... and Dorothy about that same time.

were a half-century denouement—but not bad or disappointing or depressing, as it might have been for others. It was a chosen career and life, after playing a central and dangerous part, in a top-flight military operation, at successful battles that were important to the world.

Through it all, he "regarded himself—to the end of his days—as Marine first, last, and always." ✪

BIBLIOGRAPHY

BOOKS AND PERIODICALS

Axelrod, Alan, Ph.D. *The Complete Idiot's Guide to World War* I. New York: Alpha Group, 2000.

Boyd, Thomas. "Sound Adjutant's Call! – A Story," *Scribner's Magazine*, Vol. LXXVI. New York: Charles Scribner's Sons, July 1924, pp. 32-43.

Boyd, Thomas. *Through the Wheat: A Novel.* New York: Charles Scribner's Sons, 1923.

Clark, George B. *The Fourth Marine Brigade in World War I.* Jefferson, North Carolina: McFarland & Company, Inc., 2015.

Clark, George B. *Devil Dogs, Fighting Marines of World War I.* Annapolis, Maryland: Naval Institute Press, 1999.

Egan, Jennifer. *Manhattan Beach.* New York: Simon & Schuster, 2017.

Grant, R.G. *World War I, The Definitive Visual History.* New York: DK Publishing, 2014.

Johnson, Douglas V. II, and Hillman, Rolfe L., Jr. *Soissons 1918.* College Station, Texas; Texas A&M University Press, 1999.

Keegan, John. *The First World War.* New York: Vintage Books, 1998.

Long Island Star-Journal. New York: August 9, 1945, page 13, and September 6, 1945, page 11.

New York Times. New York: The New York Times Company, 1919; date and page reference unknown.

Paris, W. Francklyn. *Napoleon's Legion.* New York: Funk and Wagnalls Company, 1927.

Register of the Commissioned and Warrant Officers of the United States Navy and Marine Corps. Washington: Government Printing Office, 1914.

Smith, Cleveland H., and Taylor, Gertrude R. *United States Service Symbols.* New York: Duel, Sloan and Pearce, Inc., 1942.

The Princeton Weekly, Volume XXII, No. 29, pages 654-6. Princeton, N.J.: Princeton University Press, May 3, 1922.

The Recruiters' Bulletin, Volume 4, Number 10. New York: August 1918, page 18.

Thomason, John W., Jr. *Fix Bayonets!.* New York: Charles Scribner's Sons, 1927. Accessed at: https://archive.org/stream/fixbayonetsoojohn_1/fixbayonetsoojohn_1_djvu.txt

Westwell, Ian. *World War I Day by Day.* Hoo, England: Grange Books plc, 2000.

Wilkes-Barre Times Leader. Wilkes-Barre, Pa.: January 9, 1925, page 11.

ON-LINE SITES

6thmarines.marines.mil/Units/1st-Battalion/History/www.worldwar1.com/dbc/ct_bw.htm

archive.org/stream/historyoffirstdioosoci/historyoffirstdiooso-ci_djvu.txt

en.wikipedia.org/wiki/American_Expeditionary_Forces

ibiblio.org/hyperwar/AMH/XX/WWI/USMC/USMC-WWI.html

mca-marines.org/leatherneck/world-war-i-75-years-ago-attack-soissons: Nilo, James R. *World War I – 75 Years Ago: Attack on Soissons*. July 1993

militaryhistory.about.com/od/worldwari/p/BelleauWood.htm

FAMILY COLLECTIONS AND OTHER

Arnold, Platt T. Family history recollections, 2018

Butler, William C. M. III. Family history recollections, 2018

Military Records for Arthur H. Turner. St. Louis: National Personnel Records Center, 2018.

Scott, Ellen Turner. Family history and genealogy documents and notes (unpublished), 2018.

Turner, Arthur H. and C. Franklin. *Notes on Family History* (unpublished), edited by E. S. R. Turner and J. L. D. Turner, pre-1972.

Turner, Charles Innes. Family artifacts, recollections, and conversations (unpublished), 2017-18.

Turner, Charles Simpson. Family history notes (unpublished), April 15, 1974.

Turner, William D. Family artifacts, documents, photographs, correspondence, and conversations, 2017-18

ILLUSTRATION SOURCES

(BY PAGE NUMBER)

TITLE PAGE | (Uniformed portrait) Turner family collection.

DEDICATION PAGE | (Cadet portrait) Turner famiy collection.

xiv | (C.S. Turner advertisement) Turner family collection.

2 | (Mr. Peanut) Mrpeanut.jpg (amf + photos).

4 | (188 West River Street) Street view by maps.google.com, © 2018.

6 | (Marine Guard on U.S.S. *Nebraska*, 1915) Turner family collection.

10 | (Taft Commission) Turner family collection.

16 | (U.S.S. *Nebraska*) Accessed at: navsource.org/ archives/01/013/011406.jpg

24 | (AHT on a horse) Turner family collection.

26 | (Wilson Commission) Turner family collection.

29 | (1/6 insignia) Accessed at: https://commons.wikimedia. org/wiki/File:1-6_battalion_insignia.png

30 | (Marriage certificate) Turner family collection.

33 | (U.S.S. *Henderson*) Accessed at: http://www.navsource.org/archives/09/12/09120916.jpg

35 | (AEF Identity card) Turner family collection.

36 | (3 France pictures) Turner family collection.

38 | (St. Nazaire to Serans map) Turner family collection/Curt Carpenter.

40 | (P.C. Bordeaux photo) Turner family collection.

44 | (Cigar letter) Turner family collection.

46 | (Belleau Wood map) Clark, George B. *Devil Dogs*, page 75.

48 | (Hand-to-hand) La Brigade Marine Americaine Au Bois De Belleau, Georges Scott. Accessed at: en.wikipedia.org/wiki/Battle_of_Belleau_Wood

49 | (4 company movements) Clark, George B. *Devil Dogs*, page 147.

50 | (1/6 leaders) Turner family collection.

53 | (Barren Belleau Wood) Clark, George B. *The Fourth Marine Brigade in World War I*, page 13.

54 | (Croix de Guerre with gilt star, Silver Star) From public, on-line sites.

55 | (Devil Dog poster) Accessed at: https://commons.wiki
media.org/wiki/File:Teufel_Hunden_US_Marines_recruit
ing_poster.jpg

58 | (Belleau Wood to Tigny map) Turner family collection/
Curt Carpenter.

59 | (Soissons map) Clark, George B. *Devil Dogs*, page 227.

61 | (Field toward Tigny) Clark, George B. *The Fourth Marine
Brigade in World War I*, page 168.

63 | (Minenwerfer) Unattributed, accessed at: http://www.
guns.com/2016/05/11/scotish-town-saves-rare-german-
minenwerfer-from-the-scrapheap-5-photos/

64 | (Vierzy to Tigny map) Clark, George B. *Devil Dogs*, page 245.

66 | (Cave near Vierzy) Accessed at: https://en.wikipedia.org/
wiki/1st_Battalion,_6th_Marines#/media/File:Scott_
Belleau_Wood.jpg

67 | (Vierzy to Brest map) Turner family collection/Curt
Carpenter.

71 | (Legion of Honor certificate) Turner family collection.

72 | (6 medals) From public, on-line sites.

76 | (On crutches) Turner family collection.

81 | (Dorothy and boys) Turner family collection.

83 | (Handsome couple) Turner family collection.

84 | (Haiti 'visa') Turner family collection.

93 | (1937 Packard) Turner family collection.

95 | TOP | (239 Main Street) Turner family collection.
BOTTOM | (1697 Tibbits) Google at http://thetimes-tribune.
mycapture.com/mycapture/enlarge.asp?image=42502788&
event=1491844&CategoryID=49658

96 | (Captain portrait) Turner family collection.

98 | (BNY GCM) Turner family collection.

99 | (550 Argyle) Google at: https://www.google.com/maps/pl
ace/550+Argyle+Rd,+Brooklyn,+NY+11230/@40.6357175,-
73.9652832,3a,75y,252.86h,90t/data=!3m7!1e1!3m5!1sXEeC
LlnT1cLUPawC6PNLhA!2e0!6s%2F%2Fgeo3.ggpht.com%
2Fcbk%3Fpanoid%3DXEeCLlnT1cLUPawC6PNLhA%26o
utput%3Dthumbnail%26cb_client%3Dsearch.TACTILE.
gps%26thumb%3D2%26w%3D392%26h%3D106%26yaw
%3D252.85803%26pitch%3D0%26thumbfov%3D100!7i13
312!8i6656!4m5!3m4!1s0x89c25b3362fe7c65:0xf1230ed3a
0a38041!8m2!3d40.6356584!4d-73.9655322

101 | (U.S.S. *Missouri* 'announcement') Turner family
collection.

102 | (BNY hospital) Accessed at: https://www.google.com/ search?q=naval+hospital+brooklyn+images&client=firef ox-b-1&tbm=isch&tbo=u&source=univ&sa=X&ved=0ahUK Ewi4wM6M5MPaAhUmVd8KHVH-AFUQ7AkIQg&biw=10 22&bih=503#imgrc=setBtroGUkAZGM:

103 | (Irem fez) Turner family collection.

105 | (Promotion card) Turner family collection.

106 | (Couple and grandson) Turner family collection.

113 | (Wilkes-Barre flood) wbflood.jpg; accessed at: http:// thetimes-tribune.mycapture.com/mycapture/enlarge.asp?i mage=42502788&event=1491844&CategoryID=49658

114 | (Barney Street flood) Turner family collection.

115 | (Color guard) Turner family collection.

116 | (2 gravestones) Accessed at: https://www.findagrave. com/memorial/31469930/arthur-hubesty-turner#view-photo=126294410
AND AT: https://www.findagrave.com/memorial/31469933/ dorothy-turner#view-photo=126294607

127 | TOP | (3 soldiers) Turner family collection.
BOTTOM | (Dorothy) Turner family collection.

INDEX

CPSIA information can be obtained
at www.ICGtesting.com
Printed in the USA
LVHW07n1919061018
592690LV00005B/10/P